PENGUIN BOOKS
BULLETPROOF

Teresa Rehman is an award-winning journalist based in north-east India. She worked for *India Today*, the *Telegraph* and *Tehelka* before she began editing the *Thumb Print*. She is an alumnus of Indian Institute of Mass Communication, New Delhi. Recipient of the WASH Media Awards 2009-2010, she had received the Ramnath Goenka Excellence in Journalism Award for two consecutive years (2008-09 and 2009-10) for the category 'Reporting on J & K and the Northeast (Print)'. Her other honours include Laadli Media Award for Gender Sensitivity 2011, Sanskriti Award 2009 for Excellence in Journalism and the Seventh Sarojini Naidu Prize 2007 for Best Reporting on Women and Panchayati Raj by The Hunger Project. She was also featured in the Power List of *Femina* magazine in 2012. Her first book is titled *The Mothers of Manipur*.

BULLET

A JOURNALIST'S NOTEBOOK
ON REPORTING CONFLICT

PROOF

TERESA REHMAN

PENGUIN BOOKS

An imprint of Penguin Random House

PENGUIN BOOKS

USA | Canada | UK | Ireland | Australia
New Zealand | India | South Africa | China | Singapore

Penguin Books is part of the Penguin Random House group of companies
whose addresses can be found at global.penguinrandomhouse.com

Published by Penguin Random House India Pvt. Ltd
4th Floor, Capital Tower 1, MG Road,
Gurugram 122 002, Haryana, India

Penguin
Random House
India

First published in Penguin Books by Penguin Random House India 2019

ISBN 9780143445739

Typeset in Adobe Caslon Pro by Manipal Digital Systems, Manipal

Printed at Repro India Limited

www.penguin.co.in

FSC
www.fsc.org

MIX
Paper from
responsible sources
FSC® C047271

This is a legitimate digitally printed version of the book and therefore might not
have certain extra finishing on the cover.

For
Kyra, Tamara and Raza

CONTENTS

PROLOGUE

It was like needles poking below my belly. The abdominal pain was excruciating enough to force my fingers off the keyboard, as I had to slouch on the chair. Holding my hand over the spot, I was forced to wind up writing for the day, its ninth time in a week. Because, as I tried to sum up this book, articulating on issues close to my heart, I had been taking medicine for a painful gynaecological condition called endometriosis and adenomyosis. 'This condition occurs when bits of the tissue that line the uterus (endometrium) grow on other pelvic organs. The endometrial tissue thickens and bleeds outside the uterus, just as the normal endometrium does during a menstrual cycle,' my gynaecologist explained.

However, I did not realize then that my uterus would literally stall my otherwise frenzied life as a chronicler, journalist, explorer and mother. A few hours later, popping a painkiller, I tried again. The clock went on ticking as I stared at my laptop, trying to weave stories from my reporting experiences. In the backdrop, I could hear my teenage daughter playing Rag Bhairavi on her violin. Shoving the hot-water bag on my lap, I shut my eyes and tried to subdue the killer cramps; like a dexterous weaver trying to untangle and play with the labyrinthine threads, I recalled my two-decade-long innings as a journalist in north-east India, a region that has witnessed bloodbath, unrest and violence.

This book is also the story of a woman trudging untrodden paths. I am the first journalist in my family's long history of teachers, doctors and engineers. Therefore, this arduous journey as a combat journalist is mine alone. A lone wolf, I had steered my way through new paths, sometimes taking the back alley to stumble on new truths. Some stories unfolded with the speed and terseness of a thriller. I also discovered a kinship with many women who worked in places where women are socially disadvantaged. I remember meeting a couple of women in Urdu media in Bihar. We discussed at length how difficult it is for a woman to take up journalism professionally in small districts and mofussil towns. There are several reasons: the nexus between politicians and media houses, lack of security, inadequate compensation, and infrastructural lacunae— such as lack of electricity, Internet and computers.

But here I was. My home turf was a convoluted conflict zone. Stationed at Guwahati, working for a national news magazine, I had the responsibility of reporting seven north-eastern states of the Indian Union. I had to walk a tightrope—without any safety gear or support system. There were many things I did for the first time: for instance, my meeting with a sniper, chasing the ULFA leaders inside a government hospital when they came for their regular health check-up, grabbing an interview with a top militant leader as he came for his court hearing, and being caught in a crossfire at a remote place in Nagaland. The difficult geographical terrain also added to the occupational hazard.

My focus in my work was to demystify the conflict, humanize it—to talk about the human helplessness and desperation. Conflict in north-east India is real. The fear is real. But as a journalist reporting from the region, I was in a constant quest for the larger vantage point—the disruption of everyday life, the untold stories of separation of families, and breaking down of villages and tradition. And, most often, I was not trained, in one of India's premier media schools, how to deal with the situations that conflict often brought forth. To work on the ground is a different craft altogether. Moreover, I had to work doubly hard to ensure that my gender was not a handicap.

The vast and diverse region of north-east is often ghettoized into a monolith; and for a journalist, mapping this terrain is a daunting task. A journalist has to face the wrath of both the state and the non-state actors. It is even trickier because of draconian legislations like the Armed Forces (Special Powers) Act, 1958 (AFSPA). AFSPA gives extraordinary power and impunity to the armed forces in areas declared as 'disturbed'. AFSPA was passed on 11 September 1958 and was first applied in the Naga Hills (then part of Assam). Gradually, it was enforced in the seven north-eastern states. The Act was also in force in Punjab and Chandigarh from 1983 to 1997. Presently, the Act is in force in Jammu and Kashmir. The most damning are Sections 4 and 6 of the Act. The former enables security forces to 'fire upon or otherwise use force, even to the causing of death' where laws are being violated. The latter says no criminal prosecution will lie against any person who has taken action under this Act. Therefore, in so many years of its being, not a single army or paramilitary officer or soldier has been prosecuted for murder, rape, destruction of property (including the burning of villages in the 1960s in Nagaland and Mizoram).[1]

The many quandaries of the north-east have been reported by writers and journalists. Often, there are no easy answers. Conflict reporting seems very masculine—full of stories of artillery, statistics, guns, weapons, soldiers, militants, peace talks and often dry press releases. The subplots, the stories of the common people, especially of women and children, are often missing. More so, a woman reporting hardcore conflict from the region is unheard of.

Can a journalist's gender be an issue in reporting conflict? A gender-specific approach to the safety of journalists in fragile security zones has been discussed in various international fora. Women journalists face additional challenges like sexual assault and abuse. News editors may refrain from assigning women journalists in difficult regions as they would not want to take chances with their complicated and expensive safety precautions. Without institutional support, female freelancers find it even more difficult, and local female journalists even more so because they are without the institutional support of rich media houses.[2] A few years ago, at a militant camp near the Assam–West Bengal border, I had felt overdressed. In acquiescence to an unwritten code, I wore a full-sleeve shirt and scarf over my neck, even though I started feeling hot. As a media student, I don't remember ever reading any guidebook for journalists to be safe at work—let alone for a female journalist who can be subjected to perils like intimidation, surveillance and threat to life.

Abeer Saady, former vice president of the Egyptian Press Syndicate, shares some practical safety advice with female reporters worldwide, based on her personal experiences, in the very handy, downloadable *What If . . .? Safety Handbook for Women Journalists*. Published by the International Association of Women in Radio and Television (IAWRT), along with UNESCO and the Norwegian Union of Journalists, Saady's book is structured around what she terms the safety pyramid: Physical, Digital and Psychosocial. She also recommends journalists at risk to learn a self-defence sport and carry a legal non-lethal weapon like pepper spray, a whistle or a rape alarm, or deodorant spray that can be used against an assailant. Travel safety has become increasingly important for journalists covering wars, but Saady noted that getting from one location to another nearby could be equally fraught with danger.

I was aware of the risks that I was taking on. But I never went prepared. I was armed only with my pen, notebook and intuition. I simply assumed that I would be safe, and that if anything went wrong, I might have to think of ways to wriggle my way out. A safety gear or bulletproof jacket did not exist for me. It's not that I was oblivious to the fact that all over the world female journalists are killed, assaulted, threatened and defamed. In fact, it was much later that I learnt that, in order to help women journalists stay safe in unsafe regions, International Women's Media Foundation (IWMF) provides the much-needed Hostile Environment and First-aid Training (HEFAT).[3]

In HEFAT courses, journalists participate in both classroom-based learning and real-life scenarios to simulate situations that journalists may encounter in the field. I had personally encountered some of these situations like emergency first aid, digital security, personal security, civil unrest, emotional care, checkpoint navigation, and reaction under gunfire.[4]

For journalists who report from under-reported regions that are away from the radar of the so-called 'national' media, this kind of safety training and mechanism seem far-fetched. I represent a dichotomy between the grounded field journalist and the media desks operating from big cities like New Delhi. My understanding keeps me from getting sucked into the controlled narrative from the region endorsed by various forces. I keep in touch with my sources, who are sometimes a domestic help, the secretary of the bus drivers' association, a nurse, a traffic constable, gatekeeper of a local college, an ambulance driver, or a pan shop owner.

In a region fraught with sensitive identitarian and ethnic politics, one can quickly be branded an 'outsider' or a 'parachute journalist' trying to steal 'their' stories. Heckled at by trolls and critics, the real test of a journalist in a heterogeneous region like north-east India lie in delicately sculpting a path that can tell real, objective stories. It's about lending a frog's-eye view of the world.

It was unnerving to read about the tragic deaths of journalists who were killed on the job. The killings of Swedish freelancer Kim Wall, blogger Daphne Caruana Galizia, American-born journalist Hala Barakat, Indian journalist Gauri Lankesh reiterate the unsafe conditions for women journalists reporting under hostile conditions. Closer home, my journalist colleague from Arunachal Pradesh, Tongam Rina, had a narrow escape when she was shot at from close range in 2012 as she was entering her office. Tongam is the associate editor of *The Arunachal Times*. According to the Committee to Protect Journalists and the Press Emblem Campaign, the number of journalists killed in 2017 was around 50–85, of which roughly 15 per cent were women.

It's an unassailable reality that journalists working in this troubled region, especially in Manipur and Nagaland, are constantly flirting with danger. In a state like Manipur, where over twenty different underground outfits operate, editors have been killed by unidentified gunmen, bombs have been delivered to newspaper offices, media houses are forced to publish press releases, and diktats are issued to journalists against doing their job. Media persons often have to face the wrath of government agencies as well, including the security forces.[5]

Press censorship by the state is, in fact, a worldwide phenomenon. Some regions hog the limelight. Among the most censored regions worldwide, Eritrea and North Korea rank at the top. More than half of the journalists imprisoned globally are charged with anti-state crimes.[6] But north-east India has mostly been left out of the geography of press censorship.

In many ways, it has been an educational experience for me to know and share my feelings with women and children who have been the worst affected. Many situations were novel. I was treated with utmost respect in the militant camps I have been to. There were instances of slight awkwardness; some looked at me with scepticism in these camps; but they never made me feel unsafe. In many cases, the militant groups realized the media's importance, and their publicity wing was one of their most important ones. In fact, I also met a couple of retired and surrendered militant leaders who took to journalism as their sinecure. A chapter in the book is about them.

In the course of my long innings in reporting hardcore conflict, I never really took care of my personal wellbeing. Reporting disturbing events and on the survivors of trauma tends to take a toll on your psyche. I was surprised as I was not aware that the repeated exposure to violence and bloodshed in my profession could stress me so much that I might have to seek professional help. And in regions like north-east India, there is practically no support for a journalist to deal with prolonged stress that can enhance the risks of difficulties like depression, post-traumatic stress disorder (PTSD) and panic attacks.

After covering a 'fake encounter' in Manipur, I had to consult a psychiatrist after I became increasingly irritable and tensed. I had to experience personal attacks, intimidation and threats, which was when I realized the importance of my personal safety and psychological counselling for PTSD. Therefore, this book is a deeply personal story, speaking also of my vulnerabilities.

The impact of the story made me an insomniac. I had nightmares. I became grouchy and started screaming at my child. I start talking to myself. There was very little joy in my life. One day, when I hit my daughter over a petty matter, my husband decided that I needed counselling. We decided to see a psychiatrist.

There has always been a mental block about visiting a psychiatrist. I remember a senior Guwahati-based psychiatrist once saying that, in the early years of her career, some of her patients came to see her at night, under the cover of darkness, because there was so much stigma associated with consulting a psychiatrist in India. Reluctantly, I agreed to meet the psychiatrist. But I kept it a closely guarded secret. Maybe I was not ready to tell the world then. However, I was relieved after a few sessions with him. He asked me, 'Is there anything that's troubling you?' I explained the circumstances to him over several sessions, and he finally confirmed that it was a case of PTSD.

My experience would have probably been different if there had been a support network for journalists in the region—legal, social, psychological. Whatever happens in this part of the world is barely noticed elsewhere. We get our stories from areas cursorily labelled inaccessible, dangerous and less important—which was one more reason to write *Bulletproof*.

1

MEETING MUIVAH

'Women have greater access to areas where there is conflict.
For instance, if there is a blast in Peshawar . . . women go
to the homes, and speak to women and children and families
of victims . . . [However, w]omen journalists reporting in
conflict areas is something new in this generation.'
  —*Mariana Baabar's speech at the South Asian Women*
     in Media (SAWM) conference in Lahore, 2009

A host of women journalists in colourful clothes set the
convention hall ablaze with their impeccable style—salwar-
kameezes, tiny ruffles, sequins and fringed hemlines. Eyes
sparkle, dupattas rustle amid soft giggles as they get to
know each other. One of them comes up to me and feels
my 'pat' (silk) mekhala-sador. 'This is one of the finest silk
I have ever seen!'

They have come from different South Asian countries.
As part of a plenary of the first regional conference of South

Asian Women in Media (SAWM), they are engaged in an animated discussion on the hazards of reporting from conflict zones. I sit with the group, still soaking in that I have crossed the border over to Lahore, in Pakistan. I replug my own journey as a journalist of two decades, as I listen to their spirited conversation.

It is exciting to be in Lahore. I am the sole representative of north-east India. As I clutch my passport at Wagah border, to cross over with a group of women journalists from all over India, I lean forward, my eyes darting to the sprawling open gate and the buzz beyond. It is a historic moment. Journalists in north-east India often work in isolation, and to be part of such a group of scribes from countries like Afghanistan, Nepal, Bhutan, Pakistan, Bangladesh, Sri Lanka and even Maldives is indeed a privilege.

It is exciting to listen to their stories of reporting from conflict zones. I remember a conversation with a social activist from Arunachal Pradesh. She was once with a team to visit the Wagah border, who stood out because of her Mongoloid features and her ethnic attire. Not unexpectedly, she was asked if she was Indian. Racial profiling is nothing new for people of north-east India; their Indian identity is often questioned; sometimes they are asked even to produce their passport. But she was unfazed. Much to everyone's amazement, she sang a ghazal by Mehdi Hassan. 'I could be even a Pakistani. It's just a matter of geographical borders chalked out by human beings,' she said.

Lost in thought, I am taken aback when Pakistani journalist Munizae Jahangir asks me, 'Do you wear a bulletproof jacket when you go reporting?'

I fumble for words and gulp some water. I had never really discussed my work experiences with anyone before. I try to identify instances of my own life when I flirted with danger while reporting from conflict hotbeds northeast of India, visiting militant camps and meeting militant leaders. I have even looked down the barrel of a gun and have had many heart-stopping moments. It never occurred to me that I should wear a protective garment, a bulletproof jacket, which many journalists working for foreign media do while reporting from conflict zones.

It did not occur to me in 2007 when I was on one of my most thrilling assignments—to meet and interview one of the top insurgent leaders, Thuingaleng Muivah, chief of the Nationalist Socialist Council of Nagaland (Isak-Muivah) (NSCN [IM]). I liked to play the game my own way— persistent and determined to accomplish the task, without really calculating the risks. I started off by scavenging for a contact who has direct access to the NSCN (IM) top gun. After a lot of phone calls and persuasion, I managed to contact Brigadier Phunting Shimrang, the person who handled visitors and media meetings of Th. Muivah.

It was not easy getting through to Brigadier Phunting Shimrang, coordinator of the Ceasefire Monitoring Cell of the NSCN (IM). The militant outfit had a military wing— the 'Naga Army', and this self-styled brigadier of the Naga Army kept me waiting for several weeks. Over the phone, I heard his confident baritone giving me directions in fluent English. He was inquisitive. 'Tell me about yourself,' he asked. I told him, 'I am a journalist with a national weekly magazine and would like to interview Th. Muivah.' I could almost hear him smile. I always sensed whenever I was on such assignments an awkward or amused feeling in others—maybe because I was a woman. 'Give me a call after two days. Let me find out his schedule,' he ended gruffly. After a few phone calls back and forth, I finally got the green light. 'You can come to Dimapur and try your luck. We will try to fix an appointment. But I can't promise you anything.'

I jumped at the opportunity. How could I miss it? Dimapur is the commercial hub of Nagaland. The trip to Dimapur, however, is not easy. I had a tough time hiring a cab that would stay with me for an indefinite number of days. I was fairly apprehensive of hiring a cab from Dimapur itself, considering the nature of my assignment. It was the local view that the area is notorious for car lifters, who would not only take away cars but also kill and dump the drivers. A cab owner finally agreed to give me his SUV after I reassured him that I would take responsibility for the car and the driver. I also assured him that I would stay in a hotel that had provisions for car parking and accommodation for the driver accompanying me. I, of course, did not tell the cab owner the purpose of my visit to Nagaland!

Finally, I landed at Dimapur, and tucked myself in a hotel named after Mount Saramati. A brochure at the hotel lobby had a description of the mountain: 'Located near Tuensang town in Kiphire district of Nagaland, it is one of the ultra-prominent peaks of South East Asia.'

But my destination was Hebron. Hebron was the name of a city in Palestine. It was located on the southern West

Bank of the River Jordan. The city was notable for its burial grounds where many biblical patriarchs and matriarchs lay, and therefore was considered the second holiest city in Judaism after Jerusalem. It was not surprising that the NSCN (IM)'s government-in-exile, called the Government of the People's Republic of Nagaland (GPRN), some 42 km off Dimapur in Nagaland, was christened Hebron.

Hebron was an obvious destination for me. I was excited to go to the heart of one of the oldest-running insurgencies in the world. I did not want to pretend to know what lay ahead. I did not know what to anticipate as there was little research to browse through. Whatever was available was very superficial or documentary. What I wanted—to understand the nature of their 'struggle'—lay much deeper.

I spent the evening window-shopping near the hotel. You could get a mishmash of absorbing foreign goods, mostly from Myanmar, in the narrow alleys of Dimapur. I bought a dress for my two-year-old daughter and a few ornate satin cushion covers depicting Chinese life, men and women. As I stood haggling with the lady shop owner, my mind was preoccupied with thoughts for the following day. The previous night, the elusive Brigadier Phunting Shimrang had sent me an SMS asking me to contact him at 10 a.m. next morning. Accordingly, I had made a phone call and he sounded stern: 'You better watch out; there are protesting villagers on the way. There can be trouble. But if you still decide to go, one of our men will accompany you from our office.' My heart had sunk. But I was determined not to miss this opportunity.

I had been camping in the hotel for the past five days, waiting for an appointment. In this time, I had met up with an old friend who was a part-time musician and a teacher. One day, over dinner, he told me about the long, chequered, but fascinating history of the Naga struggle. In 1918, at Kohima, a group of educated Nagas had formed the Naga Club, and they submitted a memorandum to the Simon Commission in 1927 to exclude the Nagas from any constitutional framework of India. In the 1940s, Angami Zapu Phizo, popularly called Phizo, gave a new direction to the Naga movement. The Naga Club became the Naga National Council (NNC) in 1946. On 14 August 1947, under Phizo's leadership, the NNC declared independence of Nagaland. Phizo was arrested, in 1948 by the Indian government on charges of rebellion.[1] After his release in 1950, he was appointed the president of the NNC, and in 1952 he tried to negotiate a road map for Naga independence with Jawaharlal Nehru, then the prime minister of India. However, the negotiations failed; the Indian Army tried to suppress the rebellion; and Phizo managed to escape to East Pakistan and, from there, to London, where he remained in exile, till his death in 1990. Meanwhile, the armed rebellion continued. In 1975, the Indian government signed an agreement with the NNC, better known as the Shillong Accord.[2] However, this was not accepted by some NNC leaders, such as Isak Chishi Swu, Th. Muivah and S.S. Khaplang. They formed the Nationalist Socialist Council of Nagaland or the NSCN on 31 January 1980.[3] It started as an underground Naga federal government with both civil and military wings. But, the NSCN split into two factions—the NSCN (K) led by S.S. Khaplang, and the NSCN (IM) led by Isak Chishi Swu and Thuingaleng Muivah—on 30 April 1988. The split triggered factional clashes. Their objective was to establish a sovereign 'Nagalim', unifying all the places inhabited by the Naga people in north-east India and Myanmar.[4]

I waited eagerly for the morning, and woke up several times before the alarm clock rang. Our car first reached the office of the Ceasefire Monitoring Cell at Diphupar on the outskirts of Dimapur town. It was a two-storeyed house in what seemed like a residential colony. I walked inside the gate and met my 'man Friday'—Apaam, a tall, handsome, well-built man, who had been tasked to escort me to Hebron. He was casually dressed in shirt and trousers, and did not seem very happy to see me. Maybe he thought that I was a bother.

He helped the other cadres unload groceries from an auto van, and made a quick call on his mobile. I kept standing as I observed the busy cadres carrying sacks of rice, onion and other groceries inside the house. Maybe they were stocking it for the kitchen. I tried to imagine the number of cadres cooking in the huge kitchen.

Apaam catches me off guard. 'Somebody informed me that there was possible trouble on the way. I don't think you should proceed,' he said. But I insisted. I did not want to miss this chance. Moreover, I was mindless of the kind of trouble I could land in. I just wanted this 'exclusive' interview with Muivah.

'Okay,' he said. 'It's your decision.' He walks in and comes out with a gun. 'Come, let's go. If someone fires, I will also fire a shot or two.' He laughed as he hopped into the car and sat next to the driver. I sat at the back. Apaam seemed restless throughout the ride. He saw some guavas lying on the car dashboard and gobbled two of them. 'I am hungry.' He grinned. The driver of the car started gaping at Apaam and his weapon; he looked at me flabbergasted, but did not utter a word, and started driving.

I was on a journey to the unknown. It was drizzling outside, and I could see raindrops sink on the car window. It usually did not rain at this time of the year, but I enjoyed the drizzle, the cool weather and the winding country roads. Our car took a turn from Green Park area and travelled through lush sylvan surroundings. It was 2007, before the time of smartphone and selfies.

On the way, I was surprised to see palatial farmhouses. 'These are houses owned by the "rich",' Apaam told me, cynically. After a few kilometres of smooth drive, we saw the first-ever traffic choke on a village road—buses, trucks, cars, jeeps with loads of protestors—men, women and children stranded on the way. We inched forward, lush green paddy fields on either side. Stranded in the jam, I took out my notebook and pen.

'When did you join the outfit?' I asked.

Apaam, a man of few words, grinned. 'Oh, many, many years ago. Maybe hundred years ago.'

'Was the training tough?' I persisted.

He flexed his muscles and smiled. 'Yes, it was. I am a tough guy.'

'Where are you from?'

'Ukhrul.'

I kept on shooting one question after the other: What is your designation in the outfit? Do you like this life? What is it like to be a militant? Are you treated like a hero in your native place? He kept mum for a while and then laughed. 'See, if you have to interview me, you will have to take an appointment.' He rummaged in his pockets and got busy with something. I tried to peer in and saw him take out a new SIM card from his wallet and fix it on his mobile phone. I realized he had multiple SIM cards in his wallet.

As we reached Diezephe village, the car screeched to a halt. We heard loud angry voices. I decided to get off the car and see for myself. Apaam looked concerned. 'Hope you don't feel scared,' he said. With the gun slung on his shoulder, he accompanied me for a while. I was clueless.

'These are *kilonser*s (ministers) of the NSCN (IM) with their armed guards, trying to negotiate with the protestors, trying to stop them from proceeding further,' he explained. I was intrigued and stared at the young cadres of the Naga Army of the NSCN (IM) who looked very young, like teenage schoolboys.

The peaceful protestors were from the Zeliangrong community and wanted to go to the Hebron camp to submit a memorandum to the collective leadership— Isak and Muivah. They resented the arson committed by NSCN (IM) cadres in their village. They did not pay heed to the pleas of the NSCN (IM) kilonsers and forcefully proceeded. I came back to the car and saw Apaam quietly sitting. I teased him. 'I thought you were guarding me.' He explained that he was not supposed to move around openly with his weapon as per the ceasefire ground rules. A few local journalists waved and stopped the car and joined us. This made Apaam chary. He hastily took a copy of a magazine lying around and tried to spread it over his gun lying on the car floor.

We managed to overtake the protestors and reach Bade village, some 12 km away from the Hebron camp. The Indian Reserve Battalion (IRB) had blocked the road with buses and trucks, which also acted as shields. On the other side of the road was another set of protestors—members of the Sema and Dimasa tribes, armed with spears and machetes, waiting to stop the Zeliangrongs from reaching Hebron. Cadres of the Naga Army gawked at us but as soon as they saw Apaam they broke into a smile. Just then two of the armed villagers approached us with a machete in hand. They looked at us suspiciously and told Apaam to go back if we did not want to end up in a mess.

We turned back and parked ourselves in the middle of the two groups. And there we were—in the midst of two 'parallel governments' of Nagaland—armed troops of the Naga Army of the NSCN (IM) and the troops of the Indian Reserve Battalion—working together in perfect tandem. On closer look, one could see the different shades of the uniform that differentiated the Naga Army from the IRB. The state home commissioner, sub-divisional officer (SDO), superintendent of police (SP), deputy commissioner (DC) of Dimapur and the kilonsers of NSCN (IM) discussed means to control the mob. As we were caught between two sets of protestors on either side, suddenly we saw troops of the IRB running towards us. In the midst of loud shouts, I started sneezing and my eyes started burning. The IRB had fired tear-gas shells on the Zeliangrong protestors in a bid to stop them, and I could see both troops running in different directions.

Just as I rubbed my eyes, I could hear loud bursts, like crackers. 'Apaam, are those gunshots?' I asked, trying to keep the panic out of my voice. Apaam didn't seem particularly concerned. Suddenly, he grabbed my left arm and shoved me into the protective cover of a bush. He asked me to lie low and wait till the firing was over. 'Yes,' he said, 'The IRB is firing in the air. A civil war has been averted today.'

I bruised my elbow. I checked if my cellphone had network coverage. After a few attempts, I managed to call my editor in Delhi. 'There is firing going on,' I told him.

He said, 'Oh God. Please take care.'

By this time, dusk had settled in. As I lay low in the bushes, I thought: Would I survive? Would it really matter? Would I be reduced to a number on the long list of statistics of journalists killed in the region? Apaam then called out and asked me to get up. Broken pieces of bus windowpanes lay scattered on the road. The protestors had gradually dispersed. I looked at my watch—5 p.m. It was too late to go to Hebron. I had to try my luck tomorrow.

～

Dressed in a crisp white shirt, light-brown trousers and brown leather shoes, General Secretary Thuingaleng Muivah of NSCN (IM) sat down on a chair and smiled at me. His close associates called him 'Uncle', while others

called him 'Avakharar', a respectful address in Tangkhul.
Two of his associates sat next to me. There was a table
between us and we sat facing each other in the sparsely
furnished room. A female cadre, attired in army fatigues,
came with tea and biscuits.

Finally, I was here! I looked around the bare room,
with minimal furniture, the room where Muivah and
his associates held court, scripted many memorandums,
hatched many plans and dashed off sombre strictures for
their cadres to follow. Yes, unquestionably, it was the same.
And the man who struck terror in many hearts was sitting
in front of me. I caught him off guard again. 'What kind of
food do you like?' I asked.

He looked surprised and broke into a wide smile. 'As
a Naga, I like pork, although doctors advise me restraint.
I also like beef. I drink not less than ten glasses of water a
day. I usually sip warm water after food with light tea. And
recently, I have started eating vegetables.'

I sounded excited. 'So, Muivah is switching over to
vegetarianism?'

He looked startled, but amused. 'Yes. But my love for
pork is too much . . . I don't have health problems like
diabetes or hypertension, which is usually associated with
my age. But my sugar levels do rise sometimes, though it is
negligible at the moment. I keep myself fit by running or
meditating.' He smiled.

He had matured from a young revolutionary to a wise
man, solving complicated equations of life; but he had
always been self-assured. 'It's not good on one's part to be
confused. When a man is certainly precise—to be where he

is—the kind of orientation which would be most correct—only then can he have a future.'

He has sleepless nights, though. 'Sometimes, I can't just go to sleep. I have to think of resolving the various cases and problems. I have to think of the situations, the future of our people. One cannot afford to make mistakes.'

It was widely reported that, over the years, the NSCN (IM) had tried to develop extensive links both within and outside India. It was believed that NSCN patronized smaller extremist outfits in the region by giving warfare and intelligence training and providing logistical support for waging war against India. Muivah justified the NSCN's policy. 'Sometimes it is unavoidable—as when we see an unacceptable situation or condition is imposed [on one], one has to resist. You cannot yield to the wrong. You have to use any means at your disposal, after having done the best you can.'

Unexpectedly, I tried to engage him in an unfamiliar, more candid conversation. 'How would you describe yourself?' I casually asked.

He looked surprised, but smiled. In his characteristic soft voice, he pondered before answering. 'This is a peculiar way of asking. I am a revolutionary, because I would like to understand things in the actual conditions, because correct calculation into the future has to be the objective condition of our present. I cannot keep living on hope. We need to have a correct basis. If I have to live at all, I have to understand the world around in the best way I can.' After a few more questions, the man appeared less guarded, and more spontaneous.

The meeting lasted almost an hour. I did not check the time. We were both enjoying the conversation. Muivah explained that they had named their headquarters Hebron after the place in the Holy Bible. Muivah was a strong believer. 'I believe in God as I know I cannot save myself. I need to be safe. God alone can save me and, through him, I can have eternal life hereafter.'

As I saw him rising from the chair, I knew the interview was ending. I quickly took out a copy of our magazine and handed it over to him. I grabbed my mini camera from the bag. 'Can we have a photograph together?' I sounded rather impudent. Mr Muivah stopped for a while and smiled.

'Sure, why not?' He posed for a photograph with me.

~

The Bible, neatly tucked in the drawer of the dressing table of my hotel room in Dimapur, reverberated from the booming drumbeats from inside the gigantic church at the General Headquarters (GHQ) of the NSCN (IM). The headquarters was divided into two zones—Council Headquarters (CHQ), which comprised the Civil Secretariat, and General Headquarters (GHQ), which was the 'Naga Army' cantonment. A common feature of both these zones was the church—an expansive bamboo structure which was open twenty-four hours. Hoisted in its front was the flag of the Council of Nagalim Churches, a wing of NSCN (IM), which had 'Nagalim for Christ' inscribed on it. Mass was held in the evenings of Wednesday, Saturday and Sunday every week.

I stepped into the huge church at the Council Headquarters (CHQ) and met Adai, a young cadre who played the drums and thereafter the keyboard placed in the church. A female cadre, Minao, swept the altar. Minao took turns with the other cadres and swept the altar twice a day and, sometimes, if it was soiled, thrice. Adai said he was a member of the music department of the church, and had imbibed his flair for music while he had been a graduate in theology from the Northeast India Baptist Bible College and Seminary at Silchar in Assam. I saw a cadre strum a guitar and thought of Pete Seeger's lines: 'The stroke of a guitar can make a nation think and get it angry.'

We came out and sat on a wooden bench. Hiisu Raomei, assistant chaplain in the church, also a graduate in theology from Trinity Theological College in Dimapur, offered me tea in a glass cup. Hiisu's crystal-clear eyes stood out. He said, 'We are six brothers. My father wanted to sacrifice one of us to the "national service". While in college, I had learnt about other religions, problems of society, terrorism.'

I couldn't resist asking him if he felt conflicted ethically—because of his education in theology. He said, 'The Bible is full of stories of war, corruption, killings, hatred. If I have to fight the enemy, I will have to use weapons.'

Located in the vicinity was a 'Prayer Hall' where even outsiders could come, pray and meditate. A passionate Raomei said, 'The church is very important to us and it plays a big role in shaping the cadres. Without it, our life, our mission and our endeavour will be in vain. We need both physical as well as spiritual strength. Many cadres

come to me for counselling and ask me to pray for them.'
There were more than twenty-five Naga Army churches
all over Nagaland, and there were chaplains and assistant
chaplains in every church.

Standing quietly and listening intently was senior
female cadre Sergeant Major Aphung Khamrang, who
looked completely at peace with herself. Incidentally, she
hailed from the same village as Th. Muivah, their general
secretary. Poised and calm, she said, 'I went home for a
month in June this year. There is no definite leave period
for us—it varies from person to person and according to
circumstances.' She was one of the few dedicated people
who was also a 'prayer warrior' of the church, who conducted
special prayers whenever there was any crisis or sickness.
The young female cadres often sought her counselling and
advice.

Almost late afternoon, I was walking around in
Hebron. My mind wandered to the vast field along the
church. There was a small department store run by the
Ladies Unit. The store had everything, and cadres could
buy provisions like battery, coke, milk powder, mustard oil,
mosquito repellent coil, perfume, confectionaries, etc. All
brands—from Colgate toothbrush to Hanes underwear to
Glucon-D to Tide washing powder—were on sale. The
normal daily ration was supplied from the granary (also
called 'quarter'), but cadres have to buy anything superfluous
from their monthly stipend, which started from Rs 1500.

Wearing a wide welcoming smile, Kainu, a female
cadre, pointed to the Indian-made refrigerator and said,
'We also have an international fridge to store cold drinks

and other items in the shop.' She was an adept salesperson and kept a register of all items sold.

At a distance from the Ladies Unit was the residence of the commander-in-chief (Longvibu) of the Naga Army, Lt Gen. H. Ramsan, a remarkably conspicuous two-storeyed concrete structure. The neat flower beds were an indication that some creative hands had been at work. Young cadre A.S. Atim from Ukhrul district in Manipur tried to neatly stack the firewood. I peeped inside and asked her, 'What did you have for meal?'

'Rice, dal and sabzi,' she replied.

There were only two meals a day—early morning breakfast-cum-lunch and dinner later in the day. As part of their rigorous training, they had also been trained to stay without food for days.

Apaam, who was walking me around Hebron, was intrigued by my interest in their life. He was stationed at the Ceasefire Monitoring Cell in the outskirts of Dimapur and joined the conversation. 'We had rice and Naga meat today.' He explained, 'Naga meat is pork and buffalo meat cooked together. It's a speciality.'

Alovi, a lance corporal from Sitimi village in Kiphire district, clinging on to the gun on her shoulders, said, 'My parents are proud of me.' She proudly showed me her weapon. 'I like it more than anything else,' she answered with pride. Standing guard with another weapon was Khonielu, another young female cadre. I asked her, 'Do you like this uniform? Would you like to dress up in a beautiful skirt and a top?'

She responded firmly, 'No. I like this dress.'

My mind went back to the interview with Mr Muivah sometime back. He had vouched for women's empowerment. 'In many cases,' he had pointed out, 'women are treated as equal [to men]. If they can prove themselves, they are respected equally enough. In this respect, Nagas are better than any other community. We have two women in our Steering Committee and some others in the ministry. We even have lady commanders. They have to undergo the same kind of military training [as men].'

One of the organizations under the NSCN (IM) was the National Socialist Women Organization of Nagalim (NSWON), which looked after the welfare of around 200 women cadres in the outfit. The Steering Committee comprised different wings like Reverend Groups, Civil Societies and National Bureau of Investigation and Financial Matters.

Interestingly, Hebron, akin to a mini kingdom, had strict rules and regulations. To be eligible for marriage, a cadre has to complete a minimum of eight years of military service. And in case a male and a female cadre decide to get married the woman has to retire from 'national service', which did not sound too empowering.

Muivah seemed firm in his convictions. But where did he see himself ten years down the line? 'Yes, one is not expected to know what will happen ten years down the line. From our side we have been at our best, as we could in taking positive steps. We want something appropriate to be done on both sides, if we really want an honourable solution.' An honourable solution meant a lot to the Naga people. 'If the Government of India is prepared to respect the reality of the Nagas, the Nagas will respect the reality of India ten times more.

'The NSCN (IM) has fought single-handedly for the past so many years. It would have been impossible had it not been for the support of the masses. Our experience tells us that our people are with us,' he said.

In fact support had been evident in their recruitment rallies. H. Shadang, personal security officer (PSO) to Ato Kilonser (Prime Minister) Th. Muivah told me, 'For recruitment, we advertise in the local newspapers. People come for the selection process and, sometimes due to the heavy rush, we cannot even accommodate many of them.' The selection procedure included medical check-ups, fitness tests, verification of character and criminal records and even academic qualifications. A graduate had to serve as a soldier for one and a half years and was then promoted to sergeant major, second lieutenant, lieutenant, captain, major, lieutenant colonel, colonel, brigadier, major general, lieutenant general and general.

Are there any punishments for erring cadres?

Shadang said it varied from crime to crime. 'Sometimes they are demoted, made to do hard labour, or are whipped once or twice.'

The office of the General Staff Officer (admin) at the GHQ felt like a normal office in an army cantonment. There were letters ready to be dispatched near the inquiry counter. Cadres were carrying on their normal duties, with a few working on computers. There was also the office of the War Victim Welfare at the Council Headquarters which looked after the welfare of orphans, widows and children of cadres who had sacrificed their lives for the 'national cause'. And where did they bury their war victims? They were taken to their native place, where they were buried with all honour and dignity.

Shadang, who was a graduate from Kohima College, told me, 'It is my duty to defend the rights of my people. I had revolutionary ideas since my childhood. When I was young, security forces harassed me; villagers were lined up and questioned.'

I looked around the whole complex with bamboo structures and the traditional Morung house for public meetings. Modernity seemed to have crept in. Shadang pointed to the construction work going on by their own Public Works Department (PWD) to build a concrete secretariat complex, which would include the Tatar Hoho (the Parliament) and the church. Close to the high-security zone in the CHQ, which houses the residence of Th. Muivah, there was the water storage facility. Water was pumped in from the River Dhansiri, and there was a water purification plant and storage capacity of around 6000 litres to cater to the entire camp. They also had their own electricity generation facility. The GHQ of the Naga Army, which resembles any Indian army cantonment, had more than thirty kitchens to cater to the cadres. It was not unusual to see cadres having piping hot 'dinner' in one of the many kitchen-cum-dining halls even at 3 p.m., during the day.

Three security checkpoints lay on the way to the quarters of the collective leadership—Isak Chishi Swu and Thuingaleng Muivah. A noticeboard there had the following notice pasted on it: 'All national workers (both civil and army) using or taking substances made of tobacco and betel nut, indulging [in] drinking [or] gambling, practising polygamy and polyandry [or] any acts of immorality against the party discipline shall not be tolerated any more. Any national worker who failed to abide by this order shall be subjected to any action deemed necessary even to the extent of service termination.'

The civil secretariat at the CHQ wore a sombre look. Pasted on the wall of the Office of the Chief Principal Secretary, Central Secretariat, CHQ, of the GPRN was the list of who's who at NSCN (IM). I tried to make a list. At the top of the hierarchy was the Collective Leadership comprising Isak Chisi Swu, who was the Yaruiwo (President); Khadao Yanthan, who was the Woshino (Vice President); and Thuingaleng Muivah, the Ato Kilonser (Prime Minister).

The other groups in the hierarchy included Tatar (Parliament) nominees representing different tribes and regions, Council of Kilonsers, Deputy Kilonser, Steering Committee including Emissary to the Collective Leadership, Secretaries and Head of Departments, Elected Tatars (members of Parliament) and Commander-in-chief of Army (Longvibu).

The officials at the Office of the Chief Principal Secretary quickly jotted down the names of various ministries of the GPRN, which included Ministry of Kilo Affairs (Home); Keya (Defence); Chaplee (Finance); Information and Publicity (MIP); Forest, Environment and Minerals (MFEM); Art, Culture and Tourism (MACT); Education,

Lota and Horticulture; War Victims and Welfare; and Religious Affairs (MRA).

Shadang explained: 'As part of Ministry of Art, Culture and Tourism, we are trying to identify the various tourist spots and invite foreign tourists to come to picturesque Nagaland.' But didn't tourists avoid coming because of the NSCN (IM)? He answered, 'It is our duty to look after their security and convenience!'

~

My mind went back to the interview with Th. Muivah a short while ago. He said, 'Naturally, everyone wants peace. But it doesn't come naturally. Peace has its own ways and means.' He was very particular about maintaining a good rapport with the masses.

'The basic political understanding is that the masses are always the foundation. If they understand us, we are strong. Sometimes I also go to the villages to meet them,' he asserts.

He travelled a lot, in and out of the country. There was plenty to keep him on the move when he returned home. He said, 'It's natural that one feels happier and more consoled in one's own land. I have the best time in my own home. My greatest attachment is to my homeland. I plan to be here for some more time.'

As our car zipped past the winding lanes in the scenic hillock, I noticed a signboard stating restricted entry timings from 8 p.m. to 6 a.m. Outsiders were not allowed to visit the restricted zones, which comprised the hospital and Signal and Communications wing. As the triangular blue gate, carved in a traditional design, shut behind me, Shadang felt that I was hungry. He bought me some of the local bananas in the small market outside. 'It's quiet and peaceful here. You can even set up your office here,' he joked. Indeed, it was quiet and serene.

As I nibbled on the banana, I smiled. It was a nail-biting finish. I had managed to get an exclusive interview with the NSCN (IM) supremo at his headquarters in Hebron. This encounter with Th. Muivah remains memorable for another interesting reason. As the interview got over, I saw him adjust his gold-rimmed spectacles. He had leaned and whispered something to Shadang, his close aide. Shadang had smiled and looked at me. I was looking around for the last time at the audience hall built in customary Naga style. As we came out, Shadang kept smiling at me. Curious, I had asked Shadang, 'What did Mr Muivah say?'

He burst out laughing. 'Uncle Muivah said, "This reporter is very cunning."'

And I was thrilled! Quite possibly, this was the best compliment I had ever received as a journalist—cunning!

2

UNRAVELLING THE ULFA

A sultry afternoon at the Gauhati Medical College and Hospital (GMCH) . . .

It's business as usual at the Gauhati Medical College and Hospital (GMCH). I am remarkably patient today. I have been waiting for more than two hours now. I lean against the iron grill near the roundabout in front of the entrance of the administrative block of the hospital. A bougainvillea makes a feeble attempt at crawling on the iron grill surrounding the roundabout. I loathe coming to this hospital. I find the stench of the filth coupled with antiseptics beyond bearable.

The blistering afternoon sun has made me lethargic, and I give out a lazy yawn. I begin to feel hungry, though I have had a heavy breakfast. It's been a long wait. I take out the bottle of water from my multipurpose reporter's satchel. It has almost everything I know I may need—chewing gums, some light snacks, a hand sanitizer, a small towel, a toiletry bag and, of course, my pen and notebook.

I check the flurry of SMSes that has popped up on my phone (these were the pre-smartphone days). Maybe I am wasting my time. I start chewing a gum. I squint at unsuspecting passers-by, hoping to find whom I am looking for. Yes, I knew they were around the corner, but where and when was the question. As I turn and stretch myself, I see a minibus, with the usual red-and-cream colour combination of the Assam State Transport Corporation (ASTC), parked near the roundabout.

Dreary-eyed, I look at the black outline of a surging one-horned rhinoceros—the logo of ASTC—that has been inscribed on the bus. The one-horned rhinoceros is endemic to Assam. The rhinoceros is also known for its thick skin. Over the years, I too have become thick-skinned, I think.

In a conflict zone, there is a wide chasm between the ground realities and the calm manipulation of them in official retellings. It is in this chasm that a lot of real stories are lost. Often journalists miss out several strands of stories they manage to report. Any good reporter's kitty has a whole range of sources—a pan shop owner, the president of the taxi association, a top cop, a criminal lawyer, an anganwadi worker, a ward boy, a chef, a gardener, a domestic help, a mechanic—almost everyone has secrets to share, if you know how to cultivate them.

And there are some people who seem to know everything. If you want to meet all of them, I can suggest an ideal place. You won't have to go through the usual hassle of procuring permission from the magistrate to visit them inside the jail,' my source had said, with his eyes gleaming. He suggested that I wait for them at this government hospital on the day when they all come for their routine medical check-up. However, when I wanted to know about the security arrangements when they came to GMCH, he smiled. He only said, 'You can try your luck.'

And here I am trying my luck. Yawn. I stretch my toes leaning against the iron grill of the roundabout. Stories about the ever-elusive Paresh Baruah, the commander-in-chief of United Liberation Front of Assam (ULFA), and his steely resolve are journalism folklore in Assam. Everyone talks of the fading old sign at the Assam Police headquarters Most Wanted List: 'Wanted on an arrest warrant, issued on February 14, 1997, by the judicial authorities in Guwahati, Assam, India, for murder, unlawful imprisonment and violation of the firearms legislation. Extradition will be requested from any country. If found, please detain and immediately inform Interpol, New Delhi.'[1] Unfortunately, I had never got to meet him, though I interacted with his sister once.

In a neat row at a parking lot with the signboard 'Doctor's Car', I see a row of expensive cars. I turn around and see a few languid policemen walking lazily towards the bus. They must have gone for a cup of tea in the tea shop nearby. One policeman walks past me, crushing tobacco in the palm of his hand. They seem to be in no hurry, and waiting for someone. I give out an indolent yawn.

I wonder whom these policemen are waiting for. Must be some hardened criminal, I tell myself. Suddenly, I have a brainwave—probably, this is the bus that has transported the jailed ULFA leaders to GMCH for their routine health check-up! Why else would a bunch of policemen stand guard for a bus? I am alert again and try to scan all entry routes. I look at the cops suspiciously. I do not want them to know anything in case they become edgy.

I look around me. I see people walking to and fro. Just then, I see an elderly bearded man coming out of the Regional Institute of Ophthalmology. He is walking towards the bus. I try a closer look. And, yes, indeed, I can recognize him. He is the senior ULFA leader Ramu Mech! Mech, aka Prabin Konwar and Sailen Baruah, was a member of the proscribed organization's Central Executive Committee, and was also close to Chairman Arabinda Rajkhowa. Gradually, he rose to be the commander-in-chief of the ULFA. He was caught by Assam Police in October 2002 while undergoing treatment at a private hospital in upper Assam's commercial hub, Dibrugarh. I had read earlier that Mech was suffering from muscular degeneration and was fast losing his eyesight.

A man is leading him by hand. I am thrilled. But I do not pursue Mech as I do not want to alert the cops. I am more interested in clinching an interview with Mithinga Daimary, the Central Publicity Secretary of the banned outfit. The person who was leading Ramu Mech leaves him near the bus. He then walks in from the entrance leading to the administrative block of GMCH. I try to follow the man and rush in through the same entrance. He walks briskly, almost running, and I realize that he is the only link that can lead me to Mithinga.

Mithinga Daimary (alias Deepak Das) took over as
Central Publicity Secretary from the previous publicity
secretary Sunil Nath, alias Siddhartha Phukan, who
surrendered in 1992. Daimary was captured by the Royal
Bhutan Army during Operation All Clear in December
2003. He was handed over by Bhutan to the Indian Army,
which in turn handed him over to Assam Police on 20
December 2003.

The man seems to have guessed that I am following
him. I walk frantically along the corridors, brushing past
stretchers carrying patients and groups of junior doctors
taking rounds. I knew that they were all inside the hospital,
and now had to look for them inside this hospital, which
was teeming with patients from all over Assam and other
parts of the north-east. The hospital attached to the
medical college, located in the Narakachal foothills, is one
of the largest referral hospitals in the region.

I cover the entire ground floor and walk up the ramp
to the second floor. I lose him! As if in a trance, I keep
walking. I cannot miss this opportunity. As I am rushing
through the corridor, I nearly bump into two people who
are walking equally fast. I suddenly stop! I realize I am
face-to-face with Pradip Gogoi, alias Samiran Gogoi, the
vice chairman of ULFA. He was also one of the founder
members of the outfit. He was arrested in Kolkata by the
West Bengal Police on 8 April 1998 and put in judicial
custody at Guwahati.

A man holds his arm and he is dressed in a full-sleeve
shirt and trousers. His shirt is tucked out and it looks like
he is concealing a weapon. Pradip Gogoi has hawkish eyes,

and is a taciturn man who hardly smiles. I know he can recognize me as I had interviewed him only a few weeks ago while he was produced at the special TADA (Terrorist and Disruptive Activities [Prevention] Act) court in Guwahati. He represents something harder, more convoluted. It is an uncanny moment. We keep staring at each other and say nothing. His penetrating look is rather disturbing. We simply walk past each other. I turn around and my eyes keep tracking him. But he does not turn back his.

Just then, I spot my 'man' again. He is going towards the psychiatry ward. Determined not to lose him again, I follow him. I can see him enter a room with the sign 'Private room'. Private rooms are usually paying cabins allotted to patients who want privacy and can afford to pay. I follow him.

I decide to be straightforward. I had nothing to lose. I knock at the door, and a young man opens and I walk in. And, there, I see Mithinga Daimary lounging on the patient's bed, talking to a group of men and women. Nobody looks like a patient here. I assume that they are all ULFA cadres (I may be wrong). All of them give me a horrified look, and I realize it was a big mistake to barge in.

As soon as he sees me, Mithinga stands up with a start. He looks baffled and probably angry. For a moment, an unknown fear grips me. I shove out a visiting card and identify myself. I plead with him that I want his interview. He is quiet. Shocked by my intrusion into what seemed like a 'secret meeting', everyone in the room gapes at me. I am not apologetic. I tell myself that I have to manoeuvre my way into the interview and, if possible, out safe from the room. I insist, 'I just want an interview with you.'

Mithinga is startled. But he remains calm. He is very polite yet firm, while the others continue to look at me. The man I had followed simply stares at me, flabbergasted. Maybe he is amused too, as I can see a mischievous glint in his eyes.

Mithinga is a poet and truly a man of words. He used to write poetry under the pseudonym Megan Kachari. In 2006, his collection of poems *Melodies and Guns* was released at the World Book Fair in Frankfurt.

'See, I cannot give an interview here. Please try to understand that I am here to see my nephew, who is admitted here. We can sit and talk sometime later,' he says, calm and courteous. But he takes my visiting card. 'Ah, I have your phone number too. I will definitely give you an interview.' In what I can describe as a very lyrical way of refusing, he ushers me out, indicating it is no place for an interview.

I can only add, 'Just a few questions. I promise you I will be quick. I want to know how you survived the Bhutan operation. I want to know if others are cloaking the truth. I simply want to know what really happened.'

Ignoring my plea, he walks to the door like a perfect gentleman, opens it for me and signals me out. I realize I have no option but to leave. He is smiling. As soon as I am outside, he slams the door shut. Bang! The noise reverberates in the corridor.

Disappointed, I wander around the corridor pondering my next move. It is a cat-and-mouse game. The stench of the hospital is overpowering and I squirm. Just then I see my man again. He has come out of the room. This time, however, he looks friendly. As he comes closer, I approach him and ask him, 'Where is Mama (maternal uncle)?'

He does not utter a word. He simply smiles and keeps walking. I follow him again. He quickens his pace. He turns around and smiles back, as if to signal I should follow him. I literally run after him in a bid to keep pace with his long strides. He keeps walking furiously. I start sweating and to huff and puff. Off and on, he would look back to see if I was on his trail. I never knew that the hospital had so many alleys and lanes, and that it could be like a maze. Finally, he enters a room, a sparse employee's canteen— rather unkempt. There are tables and benches and a busy kitchen at a corner. The man walks in and starts talking to a group of people. I look around and, to my delight, I see Mama chatting with a group of people.

Mama, sipping a cup of black tea in a glass tumbler, looks equally surprised when I approach him for an interview. He is a kind and genial man. He asks me to sit down in the bench opposite him. He asks, 'Would you like a cup of tea?' Without waiting for my answer, he orders the waiter, 'One chai and *goja* (a type of sweet).'

I try to compose myself. I take out my handkerchief and wipe myself. We sit facing each other near a window. He is in no hurry. But I am. I quickly bring out my notebook and pen. He sips tea and smiles. 'So, *aijoni* [young lady]? What do you want to know?'

Bhimkanta Buragohain is an elderly man, fondly known as Mama among the ULFA cadres. The grand old man of ULFA was the banned outfit's political adviser and one of its founders. I gaze at the circles around his eyes and the wrinkles on his cheek.

After the Bhutan operation against the ULFA in 2003, there was a lot of speculation over his whereabouts. Initial media reports concluded he had died in the operation. Later, he surfaced again, adding to the drama.

ULFA claimed that Buragohain was captured and killed during Operation All Clear by the Royal Bhutan Army (RBA), while he was leading a group of women and children for surrender, waving a white flag. In fact, Arabinda Rajkhowa, the chairman of the proscribed outfit, appealed to the king of Bhutan to return the dead body to his family. However, the RBA declared that Buragohain was neither captured nor killed, whereas Indian Army asserted he had been killed.

On 23 December 2003, the Gauhati High Court directed the army to hand over the body, if in possession, to the nearest police station so that his family could perform the last rites. Finally, on 26 December 2003, all rumours were laid to rest when Lieutenant General Mohinder Singh, General Officer Commanding, IV Corps, at Tezpur, produced Buragohain before the media. He was imprisoned in Tezpur Jail and later shifted to Guwahati Central Jail. Bhimkanta Buragohain was one of the five jailed ULFA leaders whose release the outfit demanded for direct peace talks to follow.

I decide to ask about the deadlock on peace talks with the ULFA, to which Mama preached peace. 'This deadlock should not have happened after three rounds of favourable talks between the People's Consultative Group (PCG) and the Central government. Once in 1991, during Prime Minister P.V. Narasimha Rao's rule, peace talks were initiated, but were not successful, and we felt betrayed. And there was no PCG then. This time too there were lots of expectations from the talks. The Centre should have faith in the PCG and release the five jailed ULFA leaders rather than asking for a formal letter from the ULFA chairman. The ULFA chairman cannot issue such a letter without holding the Central Executive Committee meeting of the organization and this is possible only when these five leaders participate in the meeting.'

Holding the cup of tea, he rues, 'See, this is the pride of Assam—our tea. India has no right over Assam. In fact, India's national anthem penned by Rabindranath Tagore doesn't even mention Assam.'

Just then, a man comes and drapes his hand around the old man. 'Mama, I have something to tell you.' Instinctively, Mama leans and the man whispers something in his ears. I try hard to eavesdrop but fail. The man leaves. We resume our conversation.

'If you are keen on peace now, why didn't you take the path of non-violence in the first place?'

'We took this extreme step to free our motherland from exploitation and restore peace.'

'What if you along with other jailed ULFA leaders are released and then never come back?'

This seems to have made him angry. 'We are not common criminals. We will not run away; the authorities must have faith in us. There should be a healthy atmosphere.' Just then, there is a loud clanging sound from the kitchen. The cook must have dropped something. I look out of the window and can feel the sultry afternoon heat. He keeps on harping on the old issue of sovereignty. 'Sovereignty is and will be our vital issue. Peace talks are not possible without this issue.' He talks about ULFA's massive popularity. 'The organization has historical roots. The history of Assam is the womb of ULFA's politics and demands.' He condemns the alleged secret killings of several family members of ULFA cadres during Prafulla Kumar Mahanta's tenure as the chief minister.

He tells me about the inspiring courage of ULFA cadres in the face of insurmountable odds. 'Even if the peace parleys run for another hundred years, we will never surrender. We are ready to die for our motherland. This is the most difficult time for the Assamese community. The people of Assam will come out in the interest of Assam's independence.'

I have nothing more to ask this optimistic old man. He has other people to attend to. He stands up and smiles. 'We will meet again someday.' I thank him for his time. I walk my way out of the canteen and the same maze of corridors and alleys.

Unfortunately, Buragohain passed away on 19 December 2011 and we never met again. I would since go to the hospital many times but never try to find the canteen again. The curves and bends of the hospital would never look the same to me again!

~

Date: 4 December 2009
Time: Afternoon
Place: A government guest house, Guwahati

As the SUV nears the gates of the government guest house in Guwahati, hordes of media persons, including a camera crew, try to stop the car and peer into the vehicle, trying to scan if the car is carrying the ever-elusive chairman of ULFA, Arabinda Rajkhowa. I crouch at the back seat, so that nobody sees me.

Media is agog with news that ULFA chairman and his associates are either 'caught' or have 'surrendered' before the Border Security Force (BSF) at the India–Bangladesh border at Dawki, Meghalaya. There is a curiosity to glimpse one of the top guns of the ULFA. Earlier, there were wild speculations about his whereabouts. Rajkhowa has always stayed away from public glare.

I urge one of my well-placed sources to take me to the high-security zone where the ULFA chairman, now fifty-three, and his associates were housed. Since 2 December 2009, there have been reports that the outlawed organization had suffered a severe blow with the police in Bangladesh arresting its chairman and founder somewhere near Dhaka. The impatient local media is shrieking—all waiting for their moment of glory with their exclusive bytes and visuals.

According to BSF officials, they were seen on the Bangladesh side near the Dawki border outpost in Meghalaya at around 1.15 a.m. On being challenged by the BSF, they reportedly surrendered early on the morning of 4 December. The group was later handed over to the

Assam Police the same morning and were brought by road to Guwahati.

The closely guarded guest house on top of a hillock resembles a citadel, with gun-toting policemen keeping vigil on all sides. The guest house is strategically located and is difficult to access without going through a number of security checks. As the gates open, one can see children running in the verandah of the guest house. I manage to sneak in and beat my fellow journalists to the ULFA chairman! I can see a young woman with a baby in her arms pacing up and down the verandah of the guest house. A cop tells me she is Nirola Neog, Raju Barua's wife, the forty-three-year-old deputy chief of the ULFA's military wing. She is trying to pacify her ten-month-old son who has been crying incessantly. There is an uneasy calm around the guest house as the police repeatedly buttress their security bandobast. I am informed that among those who have 'surrendered' includes Rajkhowa's family—his wife Kaberi Kochari, who is the leader of ULFA's women wing, and their two children.

Raju Barua was the most trusted lieutenant of Paresh Baruah, the commander-in-chief. Accompanying them is Runima Choudhury, wife of ULFA's self-styled foreign secretary, Sashadhar Choudhury, and their eight-year-old daughter.

Known as a moderate insurgent leader, ULFA chairman Arabinda Rajkhowa is known for his affectionate and polite manners. He is known as the 'revolutionary with a smile'. The policeman knocks on his door and walks in. I peep in through the door. Rajkhowa answers with a smile. Oblivious of the scores of anxious mediapersons and common people who have laid siege to the main gate waiting for a glimpse of him, Arabinda calmly lies in bed with a blue blanket wrapped around him. It is around one in the afternoon.

I am strictly warned against taking photographs or speaking to him. I simply stand and watch as Rajkhowa tells the police personnel, 'I woke up just now. It was a refreshing nap after the arduous transit from Bangladesh,' he said. There are three beds in the room of the guest house where lay his exhausted wife, Kaberi fast asleep. The room is cluttered with all kinds of luggage and packages.

I see his eight-year-old son Gadadhar, plump and curly-haired, walking aimlessly in the lobby of the guest house. Gadadhar is wearing a striped T-shirt and shorts and resembles any kid of an affluent household. In a gentle voice, which was almost soothing, Arabinda Rajkhowa tells the attending police officer, 'We had our food only at 8 p.m. last night in Dhaka. The children are especially hungry. My daughter is taking her bath. Hope the lunch is ready on time.'

Even after being circled by policemen all around, and stepping on his motherland after nearly seventeen years of exile, Rajkhowa seems unperturbed. Unlike his appearance in the available file photos, where he is portrayed as a portly bearded man, he looks quite different sans his beard. He sports a grey moustache now.

I recall a telephonic conversation with Arabinda's elder brother Ajoy Rajkonwar who remembered his younger sibling as polite, talented and hard-working. Arabinda is a very good swimmer, flautist and drummer. Though he had no formal training in music, he had even set up a music school in his hometown. 'Charu Gohain's mellifluous "*Rati bahi bai, kune muk kanduwai*" ('Sound of the flute that comes floating in the night air, which makes me cry') was Arabinda's favourite song, which he used to hum on their way from the fields in the evening,' his brother had said, on a melancholic note.

Arabinda Rajkhowa (real name: Rajiv Rajkonwar), alias Mijanur Rahman Choudhury, hails from Lakwa in Sivasagar district of upper Assam. Rajkhowa studied till class six at Lakhuwa Tantya High School and later completed his class ten from Graham Bazar High School in Dibrugarh. Though he enrolled in Kanoi Commerce College, he did not complete his graduation. His parents were both freedom fighters. He was from a big family— he was the seventh of nine siblings. He started off as a student leader in the Assam agitation against the Centre's apathy towards "illegal immigration" from Bangladesh. His family was oblivious of his militant ideology till he left home in 1985. On 7 April 1979, Arabinda became one of the founders of ULFA. 'He is a different league now. We have nothing to do with the ULFA. But we were harassed enough by the police and security personnel. In fact, we had the most difficult time when there was an important social function at home.'

The chief justice of Gauhati High Court had to intervene and fix his wedding date and give an interim order so that nobody disturbed them. In 1999, Ajoy, who was an employee of the Assam State Electricity Board, approached the Gauhati High Court and asked for a PSO and three house guards. This was after their eldest brother Dimba Rajkonwar was shot and killed by assassins during the rule of chief minister Prafulla Kumar Mahanta. 'We, of course, never blamed him for what we went through. But we tried to bring him back several times. We, of course, were pained by ULFA's killing of innocent people,' said Ajoy.

Arabinda, who can proficiently handle all kinds of weapons and speak Assamese, English, Naga, Bangla, Hindi and Kachin, never looked back after he left home. He wrote an agonized letter to his family on his father's death about how he felt proud to be his father's son. After so many years, his family, especially his bedridden mother, Damayanti Rajkonwar, was eager to see him. On 4 June 1997, the Interpol issued a red-corner notice against him for his involvement in a number of crimes. Out of India since 1992, Rajkhowa reportedly travelled to Myanmar, Thailand and other countries on fake passports.

I ask the cop about the person in the adjoining room. He tells me it is the room of Runima Chetia Choudhury, alias Pallabi, the wife of ULFA's foreign secretary, Sashadhar Choudhury. I take his consent and knock on the door. An attractive lady soon smiles at me.

I look at her, dazed. Head covered with her dupatta, Runima, attired in a salwar-kameez, looks every inch a Muslim daughter-in-law. She is tall and fair. When she speaks, she unconsciously breaks into Bangla. She laughs gently. 'I keep mixing up both the languages. I am so used to speaking in Bangla there.' She speaks fluent Bangla, English and Hindi. Runima makes me feel comfortable with her sweet ways. She tells me that she and her family lived like a traditional Muslim family in Uttara near Model Town in Dhaka in Bangladesh. 'We used to observe Eid and offer namaz so that we could mingle with the local population.' Her husband was Sailen Choudhury, aka Sashadhar Choudhury or Sasha Choudhury, alias Rafiqul Islam.

Her eight-year-old daughter comes into the room. She is fair and has golden hair. Just then a policewoman comes in and offers her a packet of biscuits. Runima explains in Bangla, 'We have named her Shishir Anand Choudhury. Shishir means "dewdrops" and Anand mean "clouds".' She admits that they were 'arrested' by the Bangladeshi authorities but refrains from elaborating further.

Runima is happy to talk about herself. We have a pleasant tête-à-tète in her bedroom. I sit on the chair while she makes herself comfortable on the bed. She is good-natured and has an earthiness about her. She tells me, 'I joined the outfit in December 1989. As an undergraduate student at Teok C.K.B. College, I was drawn into the activities of the ULFA, and was more of an active overground member. ULFA was not banned then and they used to organize open meetings.' She used to take part in its social and cultural activities. Gradually, as her work increased, she was drawn deeper into the activities of the outfit. In 1993, she went underground and left home for good. She met her husband, ULFA's foreign secretary, Sashadhar Choudhury, and they had a lovely daughter,

Shishir. She seems more content with her domesticity now. As for the peace talks, she does not seem to have anything of her own to say. 'We will agree to whatever the chairman decides,' she says.

Meeting Rajkhowa is a whirlwind experience. As I turn back in my car, I wonder if the 'arrest' of Rajkhowa and associates will lead to a new era of peace in conflict-torn Assam. The peace process was initiated in January 1992 but could not take off as it did not have the approval of ULFA supremo Paresh Baruah. There were conflicting opinions among several ULFA leaders over the issue of sovereignty. The Government of India was clear that sovereignty is non-negotiable.

The then chief minister of Assam, Tarun Gogoi, later would tell me, 'ULFA is no longer a mass movement. People of Assam have matured now and have realized the futility of insurgent groups. We also invite Paresh Baruah for talks. We cannot decline to hold talks with those who come forward.' He, however, declined to comment on an understanding between Delhi and Dhaka, and Sheikh Hasina government's proactive role in flushing out insurgents from her country.

The chief minister had repeatedly clarified that 'Sovereignty is non-negotiable'. But sovereignty had been the core of ULFA's objectives. Will Arabinda be able to take decisions without the consent of C-in-C Paresh Baruah?

The next day, on 5 December 2009, top ULFA leaders—Chairman Arabinda Rajkhowa and Deputy C-in-C Raju Barua—are to be produced before the chief judicial magistrate (CJM). The local as well as the national media are waiting around the court premises along with curious onlookers and some supporters of ULFA. They are brought in a minibus and, as soon as the bus arrives, police surround the bus as the media people want to go near them.

The two leaders are brought in handcuffs and Arabinda Rajkhowa screams —'We have not surrendered, we cannot hold talks in handcuffs.' Raju Barua joins him. 'We will never surrender.' The public becomes hysterical and starts shouting 'ULFA zindabad'. The leaders are then sent to twelve days' police custody and are taken back to the same guest house in Guwahati. I write my story in the evening and email it to the editor. The past two days have been dramatic and I am enriched by my engagement with the leaders of the ULFA, who for long had remained unchallenged in the state. I wind up for the day. Somewhere, another quest must begin.

~

Special TADA Court, Guwahati

I always manage to hatch a plan when I smell a story. This time, I come to know that ULFA vice chairman, Pradip Gogoi, is being produced before the magistrate. I land at the special TADA court in Guwahati as I need a few moments with him, to ask him a few questions. I decide to take a chance. I request a senior lawyer to help me. The media-savvy lawyer assures me that he will do something.

As soon as Gogoi comes out, the lawyer puts his arms around his shoulder as if he is going for a friendly chat. He nods at the policeman and takes Gogoi through the staircase to the terrace of the TADA court. He warns me that I have just a few minutes with him. I follow the duo and start my interrogation on the staircase itself.

I get hardly twenty minutes with Gogoi—vice chairman as well as principal arms negotiator of the ULFA. I had seen him earlier on television and photographs, always attired in a full-sleeved shirt and trousers. The zealous glint in his eyes is apparent as he peers out from behind his thick-framed spectacles. The first thing I notice is his walking stick. In a bid to break the ice, I ask about his health. He starts talking, almost mechanically. 'A bout of rheumatoid arthritis in 1998 has forced me to use a walking stick. The jail authorities procured it for me. I was once tested positive for diabetes, but now it's normal. I have to consult the physician regularly for my spondylitis problem.'

He has a fiery past. He was one of the six youths who formed the ULFA on 7 April 1979 at the historic Rang Ghar in Sivasagar to establish a 'sovereign, socialist Assam' through an armed struggle. His other associates were Bhimkanta Buragohain, Rajiv Rajkowar alias Arabinda Rajkhowa, Golap Baruah alias Anup Chetia, Bhadreshwar Gohain and Paresh Baruah. But, was it worth it? Is he weary now? He sounds choleric. He springs back in a gruff voice. 'No, no, I am not tired,' he says. 'The question does not arise. I have the same passion and energy I possessed twenty-seven years ago when we formed the organization.

Nothing has changed for me or for the people of Assam. We will continue to fight for our rights and privileges.'

He struck terror for many years till he was arrested in Calcutta in 1998. It has become a ritual for him to attend the special TADA court in Guwahati after he was arrested by the West Bengal Police from the New Market area in central Calcutta on 8 April 1998. Gogoi was arrested once earlier in 1987, but was released on bail when the first peace talks began with then prime minister, P.V. Narasimha Rao, in 1991. Gogoi, also the principal arms negotiator of the outfit, was a 'guest' in Islamabad from March 1991 to December 1991 for one such arms deal. He had jumped bail only to be rearrested in Calcutta.

I prod him further. How did it feel like to be standing here in the TADA court and being treated like a criminal? He peers into my eyes and says, 'These confrontations and scuffles with the police, making rounds of the court are minor things for us. For us, what is important is our goal and we don't care about the struggles along the way.'

Gogoi comes from humble beginnings. Son of a farmer, Gogoi spent his childhood in the idyllic surroundings of River Disang in Sivasagar district. Born in 1954, he did his early schooling from Bahgarh High School and later went to Sivasagar College. He is more at home in the pristine rural environ. 'But now, the whole of Assam is my home and my village,' he says. He tells me he is fond of simple Assamese vegetarian dishes. He speaks fondly of his family—his parents and his seven siblings. When he was an ebullient youth and set out on his mission to 'liberate Assam', his family had supported him. 'How could I have done it without the support of my family? But my family has suffered enough harassment because of me,' he rues. He regrets that many innocent lives, including those of small children, were lost in the numerous attacks launched by the ULFA. 'If innocent lives are lost in the struggle, we feel bad for them and sympathize with them. But it's a fact that we never target them.'

The future, according to him, seems quite bright. Five years from now, he sees a resolution to their issues. 'We want our armed struggle to end and attain a political solution through talks. That is why we took the help of a group of mediators called the People's Consultative Group (PCG),' he says. However, he cautions the Centre that army operations and peace talks cannot go hand in hand. 'We have been very patient. We urge the Centre to refrain from any kind of violence.' As he comes to the terrace of the court building to oblige the photographers, a policeman points out it's time to go. He is inspired by Marx and Mao and says his dream of a sovereign Assam is very much attainable. 'Determination is everything, and every citizen of Assam should have the mentality and courage to fight for their rights,' he asserts.

Gogoi, in a way, perhaps reflects how life is meant to be lived—no jurisdiction, no fetters—as a free spirit. He is rather emphatic when he says, 'My life is akin to the Cuban president Fidel Castro. I believe in the ideals of simple living and high thinking.'

I am amused. 'Are you comparing yourself to Fidel Castro?'

He looks rather peevishly at me. 'I am not comparing myself to Castro. Fidel Castro is Fidel Castro and Pradip

Gogoi is Pradip Gogoi,' he answers angrily as he is whisked away by the policemen. I am reminded of Fidel Castro's famous lines: 'I am Fidel Castro and we have come to liberate Cuba.'

3

ENIGMA

We agreed to meet at a coffee shop in Guwahati. For me, it is as good as going on a blind date. I am a little uneasy. It is drizzling outside and I don't like to slosh around in puddles, and there are endless clichés about Guwahati's potholes, especially during monsoon. Time is ticking away. My elder daughter is absorbed in her two-storeyed doll's house and the make-believe family that lives in it. She has given every doll in the house a name, and is ready to give a tour of her doll's house every time we have a guest. The younger one is fast asleep in her cot. I tell her that I will be back soon. She nods and gets busy with her dolls as I walk out of the house.

Journalism has split my life into several parallel streams: mother, homemaker and storyteller. My daughter is used to a mother who walks out in a jiffy, then comes back and drowns herself in her laptop. The younger one is too young to notice. My sister finds it annoying when I sometimes forget to change her diaper for hours or give her a bath when I am too engrossed in work.

I step out on to the street and decide to take an autorickshaw. The rickety autorickshaw zooms past the crammed city buses and cycle rickshaws, and the cars that won't stop honking. I feel that being a pedestrian in Guwahati is both demeaning and dangerous, especially when it's raining. From the window of the autorickshaw, I gawk at a huge billboard advertising a newly launched soft drink on top of a spanking new glass building. The ad makes me realize that my throat is dry. I take out the small water bottle from my bag and take a sip.

The coffee shop is one of my favourite joints. Back then, it was one of the few neighbourhood joints that sold good pizza and pastries. Their flashy orange decor attracts the young crowd. They had their own bakery and made one of the best scones and jam tarts in town. Last Christmas, they had dished out scores of fruit cakes. I visit the place quite often with my kids. My daughter loves the pancake with Nutella sauce, and the waiters often smile in acknowledgement. Of course, Guwahati has changed and there are a lot more places to eat and hang out now. I have seen my city grow from small corner shops along the footpath to a sprawling city with huge shopping malls. Guwahatians are fond of eating out and we see new theme-based restaurants coming up every second day now.

I get down from the auto and snuff out the water from my umbrella. The shop is located behind a row of shops. As I walk up the stairs, my feet feel heavy and I drag my wet sandals. For a moment I think, maybe this is not the right place to meet them. Maybe I should have chosen a different place. But I cannot think of an alternative. This place, one of my comfort zones, makes me feel safer. I tell myself that I have to do this, that it's part of my job. For a moment I wish I did not pitch this idea to my editor. I could have chosen to write on safer topics like culture, environment or politics. However, I feel years of seeking stories from under-reported regions like north-east have made me intrepid. Every time, I feel like I am stepping into a bafflingly new world that can open up uncannily real-life stories. Being a female journalist in a conflict zone, we have to be quick-witted—whether to wear a particular dress or to go alone to the dilapidated toilet in the woods. Often, I put up a brave front and don't allow signs of apprehension or discomfiture to show.

I walk up to a table near the window. The coffee shop has long windows overlooking the street. I can see the bustling city passing by as the moments keep ticking. I think of the questions I will ask them, and wonder how they will look like. For a moment, I also wish that they would not arrive, that I will be happy to cancel this appointment!

I settle down and shove the umbrella under my chair; the waiter comes and hands me the menu. I try not to look at him. I keep staring at the menu card and at my phone. Those were not the smartphone days, and we had only SMSes to communicate. My source told me that they would be there at 3 p.m. I am early, as it's only 2.45 p.m. I ask for my comfort drink—a steaming cup of masala chai. I like their chai as it has generous amounts of milk and sugar. I am edgy and ill at ease. I unconsciously twiddle my thumb to relieve my stress.

Lost in thought, sipping the chai the waiter has brought, I look around. A couple is sitting at one of the tables. They whisper sweet nothings as they munch on the freshly baked scones. I want to order a jam tart, but then I feel it will be too sweet. I do not want to eat anything sweet today. Every moment seems like an hour. There is a story here, I tell myself. Dry statistics do not excite me; I must understand the heart and soul of the conflict.

I spot two men in black leather jackets standing at the glass door with a chary look on their faces. I guess they must be the men I am waiting for. I stand up and nod at them. They walk up to my table and I introduce myself. They settle down, but look visibly restive. Probably they would have been more comfortable in a dark bar with loud music playing in the backdrop where nobody would really notice them. Here, they stood out. And I stood out too. The friendly waiter gives me a strange look as I start chatting with two shady-looking men, who seem unlikely companions for me. He walks up reluctantly and takes our orders. Both look slightly dazed and gaze at each other. 'We will have a lemonade each,' one of them says rather sheepishly. The other simply nods.

Both peer earnestly at me—the 'female' journalist sitting in front of them. I pretend to be indifferent and look away.

Before I can start, one of them asks me, 'Why are you interested in our lives?'

'Well,' I tell them, 'I am a journalist and I am keen to tell untold stories. In fact, any journalist will be interested in your story.' One of them grunts, 'Ah, well, we were not famous militants. Just small-time foot soldiers. Anyway, we can talk.'

I take out my pen. The notepad is crumpled and grimy as it has been lying in my bag for several weeks. I am all set to learn more about their saga as members of the Enigma Force or Enigma Group or the 'demolition squad' of the United Liberation Front of Assam (ULFA). They are trained to carry out special and violent missions. They have both surrendered now and trying to lead normal lives with the rehabilitation package offered by the government. However, their past will not allow them to do so. I can see fear written in their eyes.

They listen to me in silence and then one of them starts explaining. 'Only the best among us were selected for this exclusive group. We had to be fit emotionally and physically and be loyal to the outfit. Most importantly, one had to possess the "killer instinct",' he said. Both look physically fit and able; one of them looks like a sharpshooter. They must have killed many people while they were active militants.

And as the name suggests, Enigma members of the ULFA were an 'enigma'. Only the top-rung leaders knew the composition of the Group. Sometimes, they were made to live like normal cadres of the outfit, and sometimes in isolation. But when required, they had to take up their role as combatants in special 'striking' missions. There were several women in the Group as it was easy for them to evade security checks. Their identity was an enigma. So much so that even the hardcore members of the squad were not aware of who was a member of the Enigma Group, unless they were on a mission together. Deputy C-in-C Raju Barua headed this secret, independent group.

The conversation is engaging. As I prod them about their skills and expertise, the more vocal of them smiles. 'I was trained in Bangladesh and Myanmar and can handle everything from light machine guns to AK series rifles. We are trained more for hit-and-run type of operations. We are supposed to be on our toes all the time. We were also trained to stay awake for several nights together.'

It is obvious that both were men of few words, but the second one was also measured in speech. I listen awed as one of them talks about their operational strategies. 'Sometimes, we would put on a disguise and melt into society. Once I stayed in a neighbourhood wearing a dhoti and kurta and sold fresh local fish. I used to carry two pots of live fish tied to a stick on my shoulders. City dwellers crave for riverine fish from neighbouring villages and it was easy to mingle with the local people. Sometimes, I had deadly weapons hidden in the pots. It was a clever disguise as nobody would suspect that I was part of a "dangerous" mission.'

However, they refrain from talking in depth about their 'secret missions'. Clearly, they do not believe in exaggerations. But I continue to quiz them. They do not quite like my persistence. One of them waves his hand authoritatively. 'Let it be an enigma. But believe me, the Group was responsible for some of the major operations by the ULFA in Assam in the past five years.' I know I cannot get more than this out of them. Probably, they were trained well not to divulge much or talk more than necessary.

They look surprised as I ask them about their own security and 'professional' hazards. Probably, they never thought about them either. 'We were ready to die. We did not fear death. And we were always ready to pop the pill,' says one of them without calibrating words. For a moment, the term 'pill' did not ring a bell. I look at him questioningly. But he does not bother to elaborate. Suddenly, I realize that he is talking of cyanide.

He continues, 'After we surrendered, our perspective towards life changed. I have a family to take care of now.' His face looks weathered with craggy lines. I can sense their awkwardness and anxiety. They often shoot furtive glances at the door as if somebody would barge in and attack them. Maybe they were trained to be alert. Or, maybe they do not trust me. They would also place their hands on their waist at times. I guess they had their weapon with them. All surrendered militants had a weapon to protect themselves. That makes me even more uneasy.

This is the point where you decide to buck up. I furiously take notes. Suddenly, I get an uncanny feeling and I look up from my notebook. I can see the 'friendly' waiter leaning over and trying to eavesdrop. As soon as he sees me, he turns away. I get back to business but I can feel the waiter hovering over us. Maybe he does not think that my two companions were 'regular' customers. They just look too shady. Their black jackets and gruff shoes stand out. The atmosphere is heavy for me too.

I try to finish off the interview quickly and thank them for their time. They stand up and offer to pay the bill. But I insist on paying. One of them clearly has a smudge of fatigue on his face. He looks straight in my eyes, almost with an imploring look. 'We are now trying to lead a decent life. But our lives have no value,' he says. I understand their predicament. They are now on a quest for the elusive 'better life' and that intangible 'social status'. It is difficult to come back to the mainstream after having spent years in solitude in the jungles, engaging in violent combat with the state. It is even more difficult for their children to cope with the fact that their parent is a 'former militant'. I ask them, 'What are you both doing these days?'

Both look impassive. 'Business, we do business,' says one of them.

It is a little strange that these two hardcore militants are sitting with a total stranger, talking about their past lives. Did they feel relieved, I wonder? I realize that a close interaction with conflict makes one feel very vulnerable. I can see one of them wiping his brow with his handkerchief. They look at each other abruptly, stand up, hastily bid goodbye and scurry out. I can see them fade away at the glass door frame. I heave a sigh of relief! Both their arrival and departure were dizzying.

I sit still for some time, giving them enough time to leave the place. I look up and nod at the waiter as he gets me the bill. He does not smile that day and has a freakish look on his face. I carefully read and reread the bill to buy time. After a while, I lazily pull out my wallet from my bag and make the payment.

Once I decide that it is 'safe' to move out, I pick up my umbrella and walk down to the busy street below. The two brave hearts of the Enigma Force seem to have disappeared into thin air! As I hurriedly walk down the stairs, the tempting smell of freshly baked loaves and biscuits wafts down the staircase. Strangely enough, it does not make me hungry. I get my story.

I prefer to walk back home. It's not too far and I want to lose myself in the crowd. I switch on the lights on the porch. I can see my girls playing with the doll's house together. I make myself a cup of coffee, sit down beside them and turn on my laptop. I have to write my story. With my fingers on the keyboard, I wonder why the waiter did not smile at me even as I left him a tip. Was the waiter flabbergasted that I, a known face out there, was into a shady deal? Was he merely being cautious or did he want to report the meeting to his manager? Or was it protective instinct that made him hang around close by? I cannot figure out. I am not even sure if that is what sent the two former militants scurrying out so. That look on the waiter's face was unforgettable.

4

DIAMOND'S DIARY

17 November 2005
Time: 7.30 a.m.

The early morning breeze is refreshing. It is a routine patrolling duty for ten army personnel from the Dumuni COB (Company Operating Base), headed by a subedar. They are languidly patrolling on bicycles at Jalah Gaon in the newly-formed Baksa district. The place is located 10 km north of Jalah, around 35 km north of the National Highway 152.

The team stops for a tea break at a roadside stall. There is hardly any traffic on the road. Then they see two men approaching on a motorcycle. One of them signals the motorcycle to stop for routine questioning. However, they are taken aback when the rider does a 180-degree turn and speeds away. In the melee, the pillion rider, later identified as ULFA cadre Dulal Deka, falls off the bike. He is killed in an 'encounter' later while trying to escape.

The rider who managed to escape is later identified as Hira Sarania, a key lieutenant of ULFA's commander-in-chief Paresh Baruah. Deka was carrying a bag and the army personnel recovered two satellite phones, four mobile phones, eight SIM cards, Rs 20,000 in cash, some pistols and ammunition from it. They also recovered several demand notes signed by Sarania, with the total amount of the demand adding up to Rs 17 lakh, and, crucially, a diary with handwritten notes by Sarania. The handwriting in the diary matched with that of the demand notes. This is the story of how the diary of Hira Sarania changed hands.

January 2007

I check my phone for messages. I make plans for lunch as I finish writing a report. It's difficult to work from home as one tends to lose track of time. I check the news browser and read about a bomb being sent to a newspaper office in Imphal, Manipur. I wonder if I will be able to handle it if I ever were in a similar situation. I text my husband to tell him this. I have never had any safety or first-aid training.

I start pondering the next list of story ideas to send to my editor in Delhi. Just then the phone rings and one of my trusted sources on the other side of the phone sounds thrilled. He tells me that he has a scoop for me, but I will have to wait till the next morning. I will have to drive down to the highway towards Nalbari in lower Assam and then wait for instructions. The next morning, I hire a cab and embark on my journey as directed. I am asked to stop in between a stone quarry and a primary health centre. I wait patiently for the next call and peer out of the car window. A lorry carrying sand passes by and I squirm as my face is smeared with sand particles. I am uneasy. Just then the phone rings again and gives me a fresh set of instructions. 'Proceed another 3 kilometres and then you will get a tea shop to your right. Tell the tea shop owner that you want the book.'

'Book?' I am perplexed. Did I come all the way to collect a book—a goddamned book? What kind of a book must it be? Could it be a manuscript of a potboiler by a militant leader?

Nevertheless, I move ahead as instructed. After a point, I notice the tea shop. As I walk up, I can see the tea shop owner busy moving the ladle in a kettle. I can see boiled eggs laid out neatly at the counter along with knock-off brands of potato chips and candies. I am slightly out of breath as I hastily tell him, 'I have come for the book.' The owner stops for a while and stares at me. I guess he didn't expect a woman to come and ask him for the book. He moves aside and makes a quick call. I have a feeling that he is trying to confirm.

Reluctantly, he turns around and picks up a packet wrapped in polythene from the wooden shelf and hands it to me. Finally! I have the 'Book'! I make my way out and run to the car. As I make myself comfortable, I open the packet and can see a handful of photocopies of meticulously handwritten notes in Assamese. I am baffled. I start reading it. Slowly. Patiently. It takes me some time to realize that it is indeed a scoop! I have the diary of ULFA leader Hira Sarania.

Hira Sarania is a big name. One of the most dreaded militants, he is the commander of ULFA's 709 Battalion. His name strikes terror in everyone's heart. I haven't done much research on him. So I call up a journalist colleague who is well versed with the different outfits operating in the state. He tells me more about Sarania.

Sarania is one of the most elusive leaders. Earlier, the only photograph Assam Police had of him was an old pixelated colour photograph of him with a beard. Later a television channel showed an 'exclusive' newer version—a clean-shaven Sarania. Those who knew him described him as an ordinary-looking man with an extraordinary mind. He is 5 feet 4 inches tall and is known to execute some of ULFA's top 'projects'. He is fair-complexioned and his distinguishing feature is his wheatish/brownish jacket and the cloth bag he invariably carries. Originally from Dighalipar in Baksa district in Assam, he is the eldest among four brothers and two sisters. He joined the ULFA in 1990, before he could take his BA final-year exams at a local college. Initially, in 1988, he had dropped out of college to join the ULFA as an overground political worker. Later he took charge of the district unit. In 1996, he was inducted into the armed wing, and in 2002 he was promoted to 'commander' of the 709 Battalion. Other adjectives used for him are 'reserved', 'introverted' and 'disciplinarian' (to his siblings). His family is reasonably well off. They own 15 bighas of land and live in a typical Assamese house. He is said to be able to mingle with the public easily and refrains from attacking places that would harm the general public.

According to reports, the outlawed ULFA had re-established its presence in Bhutan by setting up at least three camps, especially by the 7th Battalion, over two years after its cadres were driven out of the kingdom by the Royal Bhutan Army in December 2003.

A middle-rung leader of ULFA's military wing, Sarania was picked and entrusted with an important responsibility—to run the camps in Bhutan. At that time, Sarania was believed to be a close aide of Paresh Baruah, the commander-in-chief of the outfit, who was then living in Dhaka, Bangladesh, under a different alias. However, things took a drastic turn when Operation All Clear was launched by the Indian Army in collaboration with the Royal Bhutan Army. It took a toll on these camps and they were flushed out by the Royal Bhutan Army in December 2003. But Sarania was determined and, two years after the Operation, he managed to re-establish ULFA's presence there, setting up at least three camps. The camps are believed to have been located in Bhutan's Samdrup Jongkhar district 'not far away' from the Indian border, an area where the ULFA had numerous bases.

Assam Police was on the lookout for Sarania. Adopting a 'traditional' method of hunting down 'wanted criminals', Assam Police had launched a poster campaign seeking information about Hira Sarania, aliases Diamond and Naba Deka, and his aide Akash Thapa, alias Saranga Patowary. The poster campaign aimed to use conventional methods to elicit information and counted on the keen eye of the ordinary man on the street to identify militants. Sarania, a lieutenant of ULFA supremo Paresh Baruah, was on the 'most-wanted' list of Assam Police. Shaken by a row of attacks by the ULFA in Guwahati city and parts of lower Assam, the authorities had announced a cash reward of Rs 5 lakh for anyone providing information about the militants. Sarania was a vital operational head of the rebel outfit in lower Assam, and his area of operation included Guwahati.

The posters, with photographs of the two militants, were written in Assamese where Sarania and his aide had been called 'palatok asami' (absconding accused).[1] The police had pledged complete anonymity to all informants. By putting posters in public places, the authorities also managed to restrict the movement of the militants. The last time Assam Police had launched a similar poster campaign against ULFA leaders was in 2001, when photographs of ULFA's self-styled commander-in-chief Paresh Baruah, chairman Arabinda Rajkhowa and finance secretary Chitrabon Hazarika were put up at different parts of the state. Then these ULFA top guns were out of the country. But this time, the intelligence agencies had evidence that Sarania and Thapa were running their operations within the state, especially in lower Assam. Sarania definitely would be a prize catch for the police and they were willing to go to any extent to gain information about this unyielding militant.

And I am holding a copy of his diary![2] The diary that initially fell into the army's hands reveals many intriguing things, including a deep commitment to his 'cause'. The most interesting claim is that the former Bhutan king Jigme Singye Wangchuck used to visit the ULFA camps located in the Himalayan kingdom. The king used to call Sarania 'Diamond' (Hira literally means 'diamond'). However, he is bitter about Bhutan's betrayal and repeatedly laments it in his diary, a reference to which can be found in the first page itself!

As I browse through the diary, I am amazed at the tenacity of this versatile militant who has made such punctilious notes despite his 'hectic schedule'. I get the feeling that, after a tough day, he is both drained and charged by making these meticulous entries in his diary. He is full of energy when he starts contemplating the things that happened during the day. I get the feeling that this diary was written with a purpose— either to enthuse or inspire new recruits.

Sarania is a true leader. His voice has strength. A characteristic feature of him is his concern for his cadres, though he never spells it out openly. He also appears to be thoughtful about and sensitive to the sufferings of his cadres. He seems to be strong-willed and capable of inspiring respect. He believes in leading from the front; and before any tough mission, he galvanizes his cadres with his oratory skills. Committed to the ideals of his organization, he understands the importance of imparting the right lessons of warfare and social responsibility to his juniors and new cadres. He stays awake even when he is dog-tired and his cadres are fast asleep.

The diary is written in Assamese. It is evident that it was written sometime around December 2003, when Operation All Clear was initiated. The diary has also been referred to as the 'Bhutan Diary'. The diary witnesses the protracted and back-breaking journey Sarania and his cadres undertook to escape from the Indian Army, enduring the hostile terrain of Bhutan's hills. He manages to lead most of his men to safety, though some died along the way. Sarania, we also learn, has common feelings of joy, sorrow, pain and agony. The diary records poignant moments of distress at the death of colleagues, some light-hearted moments with his cadres, and musings on future course of action. His writings reveal a literary bent of mind. At times, he enjoys the everyday sights and sounds. At times, he refers to the gentle gurgle of the tiny brook and of the times he spent talking to the 'stillness of the night'.

The diary, written in the most trying situations, unveils a lot of hitherto unknown facts about how the ULFA cadres so congenially interacted with the local population, never once suspecting a betrayal. He regrets strongly how he had to leave the women, children and the elderly in the Bhutan camp in the midst of heavy shelling. He writes of the dismal socio-economic condition of the Bhutanese and his sympathy for their plight. He seems adept at military warfare, and writes about the importance of small precautions like removing traces after they have finished cooking or eating in the jungle. He also keeps himself abreast of all national and international news and refers to them at various moments in his diary.

Excerpts from the diary:

Page 1:

It is the 5th of December. I have been asked to come to the CHQ [Company Headquarters] urgently through a wireless transmission message. I have to reach on or before the 13th of the month. As soon as I get the message, I apprise everyone of the circumstances. Respective duties are allotted regarding combat, camps and the task of making the workers a disciplined force.

In the last few years, in the various rounds of discussions with the Bhutanese, we have noticed a deterioration in the situation. The Bodo Liberation Tigers [BLT], along with the Indian Army, had systematically entered Bhutan to undertake destructive activities. In June 1999, three of our senior skilled cadres were killed in a place called Namlang. Even Bhutan's army had helped, in association with common people and Indian Army.

Bhutan's elite is fascinated by India's glitter. They even go to India for education as they cannot go to Western countries, due to economic depredation. India is an ideal country for them, and they are fond of wine and women. Once, in one of our camps, we had organized Bishnu Rabha Divas [a day to commemorate the famous Assamese singer–composer] and we invited a few Bhutanese guests. After the Bihu dance got over, I asked one of the teachers, 'How did you like the Bihu dance?' His response surprised me. He said, 'Your women are very attractive.' Here, even if you ask a student of class six or seven 'What is your hobby?', you will get an instant reply, 'Girlfriend.'

The king of Bhutan, when he came to the ULFA camp to meet me, said, 'Diamond, I am finding it difficult to trust my own men. My ministers, army officials, everyone is busy singing India's praises. On the other hand, Bhutan's internal condition is not very good. There is always a fear of revolt by the Nepalese people after being chased away once.' He calls me Diamond as my name Hira literally means Diamond.

Page 2

The plight of the ordinary Bhutanese citizen is pathetic. There is no market even to sell their basic produce. If they sell their oranges in Assam, they get over Rs 150. But if they sell it to the Bhutan government, they don't get more than Rs 60 or 70. Many Bhutanese say that, if this time the price is not increased, they will stop selling oranges. Ginger is sold for Re 1 to Rs 2 per kg. When we first arrived in Bhutan, we could see that they did not even know how to use soap and oil. They had scars on their body and their body gave out a foul odour. We used to spend all our soap and oil on them.

Their knowledge about the world was limited. Our cadres used to roam around, hold open discussions and gather information about the outside world. Our cadres got to know that they were taught to respect their king, that they should keep their head down and never look the king in the eyes. After meeting our cadres, they too are now enthused to look with their head held high. This has surprised and even alarmed their rulers. The life of an ordinary Bhutanese is pitiable. They cannot even afford to send their children to school. It's obvious that, out of desperation, they might some day revolt. I feel bad for them as they have to pay a lot of taxes, though their income is negligible.

Page 3

Whenever we discussed the situation with the cadres of the West Zone, we were convinced that if India attack us single-handedly they would suffer maximum damage and would not be able to uproot us. On earlier occasions, India had to succumb to our attacks. There are chances that they might attack us with the cooperation of Bhutan. Bhutan too cannot attack us alone. Though they are an independent country, in terms of resources and intelligence, they are in no way superior to us. They cannot beat us. After all these speculations, we settled on a plan of action—to be wary of both sides. The Namlong camp had been declared the head camp of the West Zone, though only two sections were stationed there. In fact, all important documents and materials were removed from there. In any unfavourable situation, two to three sections can function there or move away from there. On 15 December, due to carelessness, one of our cadres, Achintya Rai, alias Dalu, had to become a martyr at Rangjuli in Goalpara, Assam, and three others were captured.

However, we have decided to run our activities from the Manas camp near Barpeta and Bongaigaon. This camp is reachable by foot march for a minimum of five hours from the nearest Bhutanese village and over 9–10 hours—without rest—from the last Assamese village. Moreover, the Manas Wildlife Sanctuary needs to be crossed completely. We have organized our 'active' and 'passive' defence there. It isn't difficult to avoid and cross this sanctuary. In case one manages to reach this spot, one can only find a few cowsheds and poultry houses.

Page 4

We have never thought of a direct confrontation with them. Our earlier experiences have taught us that if we are in a vulnerable situation, we will be attacked. Lack of precaution will spell trouble for us. In our camp, no cadre or leader is allowed to rest for a long time. Except for the ailing and the aged, everyone is taught to endure cold, hunger, sleeplessness and hard labour. Everyone is responding favourably and in an enthusiastic manner. In case of severe hunger, they consume wild roots, but, like true revolutionary soldiers, they never forget to wear a smile on their face.

At night, we keep awake for most of the time as there is always a fear of ambush. Even when slapped or hit while taking a small nap, my cadres never retaliate. They keep calm even after 10–15 hours of back-breaking journey and carrying around 20–25 kg weight. When they become weak and are about to fall down, they are hit with the butt of a rifle. But still I am proud that they never protest. All this because our suffering in freedom is better than the insult of subjugation.

We have to pay heed to another important aspect. We have to leverage our ability to vacate our camps at any given point of time, and be battle-ready whenever necessary. We realize that, in order to fight our enemies, we have to demoralize them. We will try to stay away from our enemies, as the more we are away from them, the fewer the chances of a direct confrontation.

Page 5

When we talk of camp-related work, we refer mainly to the camp's administrative work, rations, security, party work, discussions and debates. Due to India's and Bhutan's strict security measures, it was becoming increasingly difficult to procure foodstuff. We had to smuggle them by defying enemy eyes. We had to do with the bare minimum, and had to do away with other essential provisions. That is why it was imperative to have administrative efficiency, to be able to handle any crisis effectively. All the cadres and leaders should have a healthy relationship. According to the demands of different situations, one has to assume the role of a father, mother, friend, philosopher, guide or brother. The luxuries of hierarchy have to be shed and there should be equal division of labour.

Every revolutionary soldier has to assume the role of both a teacher and a student. There were many eager cadres who could not get along with the demands of the organization and who could not groom themselves. They have been sent off. Apart from the additional duties of fighting, importance has to be laid on training the cadres to emulate party ideals and to become responsible and effective revolutionary soldiers.

Page 6

Lack of responsibility leads to the failure of many great crusaders. A skilled fighter, apart from the knowledge of warfare, has to adhere to the rules and regulations of the organization, make a distinction between right and wrong, and attain political maturity. Briefing of the cadres is the most vital job. Though I have embarked on a journey for a month or two, it is more of an emergency duty. We have to spread the message of our ideals and actions within a definite time frame, to inspire trust among our cadres and the people of Assam. I do not want to delay that even for a moment. I do not encourage talking about those who have been killed or are no longer with us. Those discussions will demoralize everyone.

Page 7

On 7 December, I start my journey to the CHQ. In front of me lies a huge task. I have no time to rest as we have to walk 12–14 hours a day. Though we have to endure hardships, we enjoy it. We haven't met the cadres on the other side for the past one and a half years. There is supposed to be changes in the party's organizational structure by 31 December. On the 10th, through R/T (radio transmission) contact, we came to know that our colleague Raktim Narzary, alias Ranjit Talukdar, was killed in Bongaigaon. The enemy surrounded him and he burst a grenade. A lieutenant was also killed in the incident. I felt sad, but my heart swelled with pride. This self-sacrifice will not go in vain.

On the 10th, we reached Deothang and learnt about a serious problem. One of our cadres Rudra Haloi had been killed with a kukri by the Bhutanese and an Indian patrolling party. They ran away with his gun. In the Deothang camp, a spy entered in the guise of a lunatic.

At eleven in the morning, we advanced to zero point. The glare of the army officer made me uneasy. It was as if he would swallow us. After walking for an hour, Daimary sir came to see us and we sat on the grass for an hour. At the same time, we met the army officer again. They must have thought that if we had been one or two, maybe we too would have met the same fate as Rudra Haloi. But we were prepared for any counter-attack.

Page 8

Till now, our leaders are not certain whether we should retaliate or not. They wanted to investigate whether the Bhutanese really betrayed us.

Page 9

As soon as I reached, he told me about the situation. I can feel that the minister's intentions are not good. The intelligence chief, a major, came with an associate to the CHQ. He informed us that the king is expected to reach at around 8 a.m. He brought bottles of vitamins and a basket of oranges for father. It seems on earlier occasions too the king had sent things to father.

I start organizing the service records of the boys by afternoon. I can suddenly hear the 'dhoom dhoom' sounds of an LMG [light machine gun]. I ran and reached [Daimary] sir's house. I asked, 'Sir, did you hear anything?' Whether it was real or a joke, I could not decipher. I immediately rushed and took the kitbag containing arms and equipment and took the others to a safer location.

Page 10

I went to the CHQ. It was a plain field with not many trees around. Meanwhile the sounds of the mortar made branches of trees fall off. After taking sir to a safer distance, we stopped. Diganta, Mridul and *bhatija* [nephew] had not yet reached. Meanwhile, a severe mortar attack started and the crowd started running. Since the area was open it was easy to see the mortar. As they started moving, they reached a different spot. A mortar's splinter came and hit a cadre. At a distance of 1 foot from me, Liberation screamed— 'Sir, it has hit me on the chest.' Immediately we went down holding each other. After going a few steps forward, my head was also hit by a piece of mortar. I slowly touched the wound; it was not grievous but blood was oozing and there was swelling.

I told Liber [Liberation] softly: 'I am also hurt. Don't worry, keep walking.' After going for about ten minutes, Liber could not proceed further. Seeing no way out, I took the provisions in his custody and hid it in a good place under a stone. I told him that we will come and take it after the shelling subsides. We wanted to shake hands while leaving, but he [Liber] repeatedly pleaded—'Take me. I do not want to die in the hands of the enemy.'

We all have a lot of affection for Liber, so we told him not to worry as everything would be fine. For the last time, I tenderly took his hand and let him sleep on earth's lap. After an hour, our main group met. By afternoon, the shelling at the CHQ reduced. We waited till the camp was searched. Meanwhile heavy shelling

was going on in the GHQ and communication with all
the camps were disrupted. We did not anticipate the
attack.

Page 11

By noon, the remaining cadres cautiously walked to
the CHQ. We were waiting for the decision of the
authorities: whether to fight or not to fight. When we
reached the spot where we had left Liberation, we sent
two cadres, bhatija and Dhritiman, to take care of him
and we proceeded. We met a group at the outpost and
started taking stock of the situation. In the CHQ we
saw that our organization's flag had been removed and
Bhutan's national flag was hoisted.

In father's house they had written—Bhimkanta
Buragohain, political advisor.

They even took away the packet of biscuits, money
bags, small tapes, radio and personal belongings along
with the pistols, guns and bullets. Near the flag, we hung
a *gamocha* [traditional Assamese towel]. The cadres were
eager to meet their families.

As soon as we reached the CHQ school, we could
see bhatija coming with Liber on his back. As soon as
he came closer he said, 'Ankur is gone.' We were all
stunned. When he was in Assam, he was called Ankur.
Ever-smiling, he was adept both in warfare and music,
and was never behind anything. We have lost Liber on
the first day itself.

Page 12

I remember an incident on 31 December 2002, when I had gone on an operation. Keeping the main troop at the front and the operation group at the back, I advanced further. After a while, we got to know there was an accident. I came and saw a guard bandaging Liberation's ears. As soon as I came, Liber smiled. 'My ears are gone.' Shelling started again and every sound of shelling scared us.

Page 13

Father has not reached. There was no way of escape from there. Everyone has to be removed from there as soon as possible. At this point of time, we did not think much. We repeatedly informed Neog sir to think and come to a decision. The more we delayed, more the risk of danger rose. From the nature of the attacks, we were convinced that they did come for direct confrontation but maintained a distance. Otherwise there will be no option but to commit suicide. They will not let us go easily. They will try to inflict maximum damage and break our backbone. A traitor has no sympathy or empathy.

The Zone's inability to take a decision is troubling us. Repeated attempts to contact the authorities have failed. If the main person is not present, it's very difficult. In both the CHQ and GHQ, there is a lot of scope to surround and trap us. Our enemy may be sitting on the escape routes. It's crucial to have an able leadership in such moments.

Shelling started once again. We did not get time to think much. Looking at the nature of the shelling, we could conclude that they were hell-bent on finishing us. Incessant shelling started at our camp. We did not get time to think of food, etc. We sat in defence to bail out the main group as the road was not easy.

Page 14

The loud noise of the shelling intensified. Before noon we reached the main camp. We kept sending reports to the higher authorities. No decision was taken till late afternoon. Eight members of our group suffered injuries while trying to procure food. The C-in-C informed that they could not do anything now as negotiations with Bhutan was almost over. Till now, there was no order to retaliate.

Many of our cadres suggested that we leave the place as it was. Everyone agreed that it was important to save one's life as it wasn't easy to fight them. That's why I searched for an opportune place and told everyone to wait for sir [perhaps a reference to Mr Neog]. Even going to Assam and settling in at a favourable place will be a huge risk. It's not easy for the women, children and elderly. Instead, sir suggested that we wait for some more time. I looked at the faces of my colleagues to gauge what they were thinking. Otherwise, we would have to embrace death like this.

I addressed everyone, including the women and children, and told them that we would have to embrace death if necessary. There was silence for some time. I examined their faces. It's difficult to paint a picture of the crucial moment, a pathetic moment. On many people's faces were signs of helplessness and uncertainty. Many still had hope that somebody would come and save them.

Page 15

I feel I have lost my capacity to see eye to eye with them. It is unbearable to look at the children as they do not even know what their future holds for them. Several thoughts come to my mind after watching them silently. In my revolutionary life, I have never faced such a helpless situation. We had prepared ourselves for bigger mishaps, but a situation like this is unpredictable. If I say anything, people will say I am a coward or a deserter. The thought of living with such a scandal did not come to my mind. Still it was better to do something than to sit idle. I said, 'Sir, do not worry, I will take you. If I cannot come back, we will try able means to resume our revolutionary struggle more earnestly. After making up for the damages, we will teach a lesson to our enemies. Father [perhaps Bhimkanta Buragohain], give us your blessings and let us go.'

Page 16

Taking farewell from Bagh sir for the last time, I requested him not to surrender. If you are caught they will hand you over to India. If India gets you, they will finish all your hopes to do something. For the sake of the community, bear this trouble. If not possible to take arms with you, hide them somewhere. I will come later and pick it up.

After taking farewell from Neog sir, I came near Rabin Handique. Sir tells me in my ears, 'Sarania, in this old age, I have no will to be caught by the enemy. Please do not forget me.'

After this, I looked at the rest of the people with me and my heart trembled. I have experienced many such moments of farewell with my co-fighters. But this farewell seemed final. I felt like I was bidding them farewell, never to see them again. Borbora hugged me and said he would return in two days' time. Mrinal Rajkhowa also came and hugged me. Looking at their faces, I was prepared to take on the enemy forces with double gusto. I felt bad that I was leaving the battlefield so easily. I was forced to leave everyone at the *chakravyuha*. I bid farewell for the last time and told them, 'If possible, I will see you very soon.' I did not have the heart to turn back again and look at them. We started moving and when we were around 100 metres from the CHQ, I could witness attacks from all directions. They were burning houses and the provisions.

Page 17

We decided to wait till they moved away. We were supposed to move towards the east of the CHQ. By another half an hour, it would get dark. There is no sign of them moving away. We then decided to retreat and I briefed everyone about their responsibilities and duties. We turned south-east of the CHQ. Walking for nearly an hour, we couldn't approach the right direction. Moreover, the dry bamboo breaks and makes noise as we walk. We realized we were making a lot of noise. The enemy couldn't hear us because of the sounds of the raging fire. We stopped at a safe place and at a comfortable distance from them.

The night was disturbing again. The mortar sounds reverberated at a distance. We felt that whoever might have been left behind would be finished. We presumed that they would start shelling towards us too. At that moment, our sense of pain, anger and sympathy for our fellow men started simmering. Each one of us vowed that even if it took 100 years, we would take revenge against India and Bhutan. Early morning on the 18th, we resumed our journey. We got up and saw that there were no signs of their leaving. They started burning camps again. Moreover, it was not possible to establish contact with the CHQ and GHQ. We all felt very sad. The assumption was that maybe everything was over. I delivered a short speech to my co-fighters. We did not know what happened last night. It was not possible to move with the elderly, children and the women. Wasting one night meant our return would be delayed by another two days. And they were supposed to wait only two days for us.

Page 18

That is why we wanted to go to our motherland and continue fulfilling our obligations and put up a tough fight. In this endeavour, all my co-fighters supported me. I said, 'In our group, at least two should avoid the enemy. In case we face them, we will fight. We have nothing new to lose except our lives.' We resumed our journey. We started walking from the Middle Zone. Some went to inspect the enemy side. While they were coming back, they met Gobinda Baishya on the way. Baishya came to us and said, 'When they first started attacking, they did not cause much damage. It was difficult to shift the women and children under the sharp eye of the enemy.' Then again, Baishya's wife Rupali was pregnant. They had, with great effort, started moving ahead and the situation helped them. They all spoke of the crucial moment when every route had been shut down. Within two days, the women, children and the elderly surrendered to the Bhutan authorities. We sat together again and reiterated our tough future plans.

Page 19

He told me softly, 'I don't know if we will ever meet again. But one day or the other, we will settle scores.' By the evening we reached Jeraipani near the Bhutanese army camp. We tried to inspect the area from a distance. On our way, we could see mortar remains. We had to tread carefully and inspect everything on the way. That's why an hour's route took us more than five hours. We could rest only for a brief period on the road. We had rice powder (*pitha guri*) with sugar and water. I still had fried rice powder (*khandou*) for another 5–6 days.

We started moving again after dusk set in. We lay low when we saw an army Shaktiman truck coming our way. Meanwhile, the face of the cadres became serious and they regained their mental strength. I patted one's back and told him, 'Our day will come one day.'

I again recalled those farewell moments. On the way, I saw an army vehicle. We had to cross them and there was no way to avoid them. In case we fought them, we could only meet death. We carefully crossed the river and came to an open stream and sat down quietly. The rest followed me.

Page 20

I asked everyone about the village. They told us that, though it is in the interiors of Bhutan, it was comparatively safe. I was not satisfied. I sent four of them to look for a safer place on top of the hill. At the same time, amidst the sound of stones and pebbles, I could see three men coming towards us. As they came closer, I shouted 'halt'.

They said, 'It's us. NDFB [National Democratic Front of Bodoland]'. We called out and asked them to come closer. We had initially thought they were our men. They were also a four-member group. On the day of the incident [the camp attacks (?)], after having food, their commander had gone out, which was when the firing had started. There is no news of their commander and nobody knows what happened to him. They took shelter near the river and followed us. They informed us that the army was ambushing and firing along the banks of the river.

At night, we reached a village in Shilling. The stillness of the night was broken by gunshots. With binoculars we could see heavy firing going on. Amidst the bullets, we scrambled and lay low and moved towards the river-bank. First, I arrived and the rest followed me, except two cadres who did not turn up. One of the cadres of NDFB also did not turn up. We waited for them in the stillness of the night.

Page 21

For me everything is new. In two days' time, we lost two of our dear cadres and our hopes started dimming. After waiting for them for quite a while, we lost hope. We decided to cross the river. I started once again. 'Dear co-fighters. All of you must have realized how dangerous our journey is. We lost two of our men right at the beginning. We have even tougher times ahead. Still we will not look behind. Our enemies should not be able to catch us alive. Our seniors in Kachin and Nagaland have endured tougher problems. The history of any revolution is a tough story. There are lots of examples in this world which are worse than this. There is no reason to be demoralized. Our fate cannot be worse than theirs.' My co-fighters were getting a little edgy. I told them about my decision. We were hardly 300 metres away from our enemies. These two nights were crucial. If we slept in these two nights, we would have to face our enemies' 'Tandav' once again.

On the west side, the current of the River Kawoipani was very swift. Moreover, with our arms and ammunition, there were heavy bags, of 20–30 kg, on each shoulder. There, the number of persons who did not know how to swim was more. It was bitterly cold too. After crossing the river, we reached the GHQ.

Page 22

Ambush patrolling will always be there. There are no loopholes. Even if we reach Assam, there will be the army camps at Guabari, the brigade camp at Tamulpur. There is no time for thinking, but it is difficult to forget our dear co-fighters whom we lost earlier. When we hide, there are fewer chances of our enemies seeing us, and we can avoid coming face-to-face with enemy soldiers. As I finished my speech, everyone seemed to agree with my decision. This was the time for mutual understanding and regard for the senior's decision. After spending the night, two of them had been sent to seek out a favourable spot. One went to fetch water. In the morning, we got water from the field and made arrangements for food.

Page 23

Amidst the gunfire, I gave strict instructions to refrain from making any kind of sights and sounds—like burning fire or sneezing, etc. Even a slight sound could spell trouble for everyone. During the day, except to pass urine and stool, nobody could go out. It seemed like the longest day of the world. As night set in, the sounds of guns boomed again and we could start proceeding.

Page 24 [Flashback and light moments]

On certain occasions, enemy gunfire struck fear in our hearts. In between, many thoughts engulf me. I keep remembering the ones I left behind. The thought of Liber keeps troubling me. I recall the day when we had stayed as a guest at a house in a Bhutanese village. My physical condition was bad. My feet were swollen and blisters were bursting and my joints aching. I was extremely restless. Whether it was fever or hunger, I could not make out. Without washing my hands or feet, I threw the kitbag away and lay on the plastic and dozed off to a deep slumber. Slowly the boys washed my hands and feet. I called Liber, 'Please massage my body or I will die.' The massage was always done by Liber. If the others do the massage, it becomes more painful.

Dipak was on vigil, and *pahalwan* [wrestler] and bhatija were preparing the meal. They were both discussing their experiences in the field. In between they would say, 'Betrayer, cruel man' and start giggling in hushed tones. I got suspicious and cried out, 'You naughty boys. What are you talking about?'

Liber laughed out loud. He told me the real story. Back in Assam, one day, bhatija and Dutta, another cadre, were staying at a person's house. As they were about to take their meal, the man took his daughter to school. The man's wife, in the guise of serving food, stood on the doorway and looked at Dutta, and started crying. 'Betrayer, cruel man. Betrayer, cruel man.'

Bhatija, though he may look stupid, has sharp ears. He could see poor Dutta was quiet uneasy. After the meal, bhatija asked Dutta, 'What happened, Dutta sir?'

Dutta said, 'Don't make mistakes like me. You will also meet the same fate.' Bhatija, the smart fellow that he is, later found out that the lady was once Dutta's beloved.

While she was waiting for Dutta, her family had married her off to another man.

Page 25

Dusk was setting in. I asked everybody to get ready. For three days we did not have proper food. My companions had become quite weak. Except for essential items, I had asked them to hide everything else. In the evening, I came out of the shelter and addressed everyone, 'Dear comrades. Our time has come. The enemy will fill all the loopholes in our route to escape. Yesterday, you have seen all army vehicles lined up. This is why today, by any means, we will have to cross this enemy bastion. If we come face-to-face with our opponents, we will have to fight. If they attack, we will have to retaliate.'

We started the journey again. We carefully crossed the river and went back to the spot where we were attacked on previous occasions. We started climbing the steep mountain and kept slipping back. There was a big rock at a small distance. So, we proceeded to the other end. At a small distance was the Kangthak bridge. After climbing one by one, we reached a plain area and rested for a while.

The back-breaking journey started again. At a distance was a long road. We had a feeling that there was someone there. Seeing the signs of danger, we tried hurriedly to return from the place. It wasn't easy to cross the deep, dark forests. Fear, anxiety and hunger had affected our companions. After proceeding for a while, we realized that we were going in the wrong direction. After a while we heard sounds of AK-47 and LMG again. It was almost as if they fell on us. We were almost at the back of Mithinga's camp.

Page 26

After walking for an hour, I asked everyone to stop, and said, 'We will rest here for the night.' At night, we felt like we had diverted from our route and we might meet the army once again. But going back might have been dangerous. This was why everyone had saved food for two days—biscuits, rice powder, bread. Everyone walked to their groups. Some kept vigil, and the rest went to sleep. After a while, the boys were fast asleep, and there was a stillness. Though I tried to sleep, I kept waking up, startled even at the sound of a falling tree branch. Instinctively, I brought my gun closer.

The CHQ seemed quiet but the silence was eerie. The gunshots seemed to come down. The sweet memories of camp days kept coming back to us. In the midst of all the suffering, we had enjoyed a lot. The conversations revolved around a whole lot of things, including Assam's shameless politicians.

Once, while we were at the CHQ, there was the attack on the WTC [World Trade Center] tower in the USA. We all had praised this act of heroism. A country like the US, which had bossed over the world, was trying to be everybody's guardian, subjugating everyone. This attack had hit right at the heart of the USA. But we had nothing to like or dislike about this act. Though there was an element of heroism in the act, people like us who believe in the 'freedom struggle' should not be happy at such acts. In the entire north-east, Indian freedom fighters had been termed as terrorists.

Page 27

Suddenly one screamed, 'Sir, he is coming. He is coming here.' I sat up with a start and looked around. Pahalwan had seen a dream and was talking in his sleep. I slapped him hard and he kept quiet.

The night seemed like the longest night. I tried to sleep at the latter part of the night. In the morning, I heard Dipak's voice and woke up. Without opening my eyes, I said, 'Let there be more light before I wake up.'

Then Dipak said, 'It's quite bright and sunny now. Look at the CHQ at the other end. We are in an open space.' We hurriedly got ready for the long day ahead.

Page 28

Everyone got ready with arms, ammunition and our kitbag. Our journey started once again. Everyone started taking their positions. It was 19 December. After an hour, we took rest at an appropriate place. We had the rice powder and biscuits we carried with us. After that we heard the news on the radio of father being hurt and women and children being killed.

The mortar attacks had started after we left. Our worst fears had come true. It was difficult to implement strict instructions on safety on the elderly, women and children. Handique sir always kept coughing. The kids screamed and ran around?

Our heart was broken. Every time, the poignant moments of farewell kept coming back to our mind. It was a difficult time. One hour passed and it seemed like a whole day. I told everyone that we couldn't have got the right picture now. In case everything was over, we would have to take stock of the situation.

I told them, 'Let's start our journey before the enemy starts marching in the adjoining places.' At many places, we had to hold on to plants and creepers, and some of us kept slipping down. Dipak's condition was bad. He was tall and sturdy and required food in larger quantity.

Page 29

We have to reduce Dipak's burden. I even rebuked him. Later I put him in front of me. At noon, we saw a dry stream. We decided to sit and eat. After 3–4 hours, we felt that we would soon reach Assam. After some time, we heard sounds of a woodcutter. After forty-five minutes we stopped near a stream to have food. Because of not having adequate good food, our boys had become weak. They wouldn't be able to fight the enemy. We started cooking with tiny twigs, as the sight of smoke might spell trouble for us.

We had dry fish and started cooking. We asked two groups to keep vigil in different directions. We laid the plastic under a tree's shade, and, with the bag as a pillow, I try to sleep. The sun was about to set. Helicopters were traversing every moment, and with the sound of bullets and huge army trucks, it almost seemed like a war zone, though no formal announcement was made.

This was part of an unethical war, as righteous people like father couldn't imagine that the king of Bhutan, who used to send him vitamins with so much affection, would suddenly turn into Aurangzeb. Whatever they may feel, we are not enemies of Bhutan. Our organization had done no harm to the interests of Bhutan. Many Bhutanese girls were desperate to marry our cadres, though it was prohibited for the boys. In fact, many were punished severely for developing illicit relationships with Bhutanese girls.

Page 30

There was a lot of scope for revolt among the Bhutanese, but we never instigated anyone. The Nepalese too sought our help to attack the Bhutanese but stopped as they got no support from us. We knew that if anything were to happen, the blame would fall on us. The complaints against our cadres by the Bhutanese were dealt with very seriously, and careful investigation was undertaken. We punished our boys even for minor crimes like plucking someone's oranges.

If we had tried to harm the Bhutanese, they would have never got this chance of betrayal. We trusted them so much that we set up schools for their kids. Women and the elderly started staying there. As per their directions, camp and cadre strength was reduced. That was why the Bhutan king and his coterie's political scheming was nothing but mere dictations by the Indian government. They had used us, and sold us like food and beverages and took money in return. There is no doubt that the Bhutan incident had damaged us but our backbone is still intact. During our stay in Bhutan, we had led normal lives with no fear of security. There, we were more involved in social and administrative work and had started losing revolutionary fervour. This became a headache for a middle-level worker like me. Our social behaviour had changed, and we became more relaxed. I felt it would be difficult to combat the enemy in such circumstances.

Page 31

But the Bhutan incident filled our cadres with fierce anger. And this anger could be utilized to give a fitting reply to our enemies. Meanwhile food was ready. After four long days we ate properly. The aroma of the food was appetizing and everyone looked like they would jump at the food. But they were all revolutionary soldiers. For them, four days of starvation was nothing. They had been taught to resist hunger and maintain discipline. I was feeling bad for them too. They were once the beloved of their families. Some of them were young, some old. Maybe someone's mother or sister was still waiting eagerly for news of their brother or son on the radio. I cooked some more rice so that they could satisfy their hunger and be ready for enemy attacks. Meanwhile, the sun was setting and, after hurriedly finishing the food, we removed all signs of cooking so that the enemies couldn't make out we were there.

After going to the stream, we started climbing the mountain again. After walking for nearly two hours, we reached the last hill of Assam. We tried to visualize what direction would be the best to climb down. Nobody recognized these places. Whoever knew these places, we had lost them midway.

We climbed down the left side. The woodcutter had set up a camp a few days back. There was no sign of the enemy. On the open sand near the stream, we saw a herd of wild buffalos. Seeing us, some screamed and ran to the woods. We kept walking and they realized that we were not their enemy. We crossed the stream and walked amidst the woods. Meanwhile, it was getting dark and it was still a long way to the village.

Page 32

We knew it wasn't proper to enter a village without knowing anything. But it wasn't possible to walk in the forest at night either. We decided to spend the night near the stream. The river was in spate and could be seen at a distance. If the enemy came, we would be at an advantage.

After tea, we decided to cook food for the next day. Burning a fire during the day near Assam was dangerous as army camps are located nearby. After cooking, everyone had food and went to sleep. But for me, another sleepless night had started. When they had to endure hard labour, the boys slept like logs. But I couldn't sleep. I sat up at midnight sometimes. I read a book or sat in the open sky and talked to the night.

Sometimes I went off to sleep and the thought of the ones left behind kept coming back. While massaging my feet, bhatija used to say, 'Sir, we should go through Assam, otherwise we will not survive.'

I laughed and said, 'This time, while going back, I will show you Nalbari [a district in Assam].' And strangely enough the incidents were taking us towards Assam. I reflected on the past incidents and thought of the future course of action. From the 16th itself, I had lost touch with our authorities and other cadres.

Page 33

My first task is to establish contact with the authorities, through any means, and then establish contact with the cadres all over. It is difficult to get a clear picture under such dangerous situations. We have to be very careful while mingling with the common people. During the Bhutan war, many of our cadres were at a loss. For years, they had been away from the war zone, in a peaceful ambience. The revolutionary fervour was missing. There was enough scope for us to use Bhutan for Assam's armed struggle, but, due to lack of calculation and proper planning, we had to pay for it. The anguish will continue to trouble us from time to time.

We had assumed that Bhutan was a safe base to attack Assam. But, by the year 2000, Prafulla Mahanta's betrayal brought immense hardships for us. We had to shift lower Assam's main activities to Bhutan. The cadres in Assam became easy prey for the enemy forces. The workers, well-wishers and all progressive thinkers became victims of secret and open killings. In Assam, the fear prevails. The news of the demise of our co-fighters could not even be delivered to our organization. We were busy with other things in Bhutan. At this moment of crisis we could not help our cadres. We are burning with anger.

Our base has become weak. With limited arms and ammunition, we have embarked on our journey to Assam. If we continue to stay in the Bhutan border, we will be sandwiched in the attacks. We should hoodwink our enemies and organize ourselves at a favourable place. Together, we emphasized the right use of arms. It is a difficult time for us. The doors of Bhutan are closed for us. It is difficult to go to Bhutan secretly. The Hindus there still think someone from across the border will save them.

Page 34

To think that people of another religion will help them is foolish. Moreover, the Indians continue to bully them. The international situation is not very favourable. It is difficult to work from Myanmar. It is a two-hour journey to the nearest Assam village. From earlier night's firing, we could make out the enemy bases. Still we had to be wary of ambush and patrolling, and decided to proceed during the daytime. Later, we heard sounds made by woodcutters. We now decided that it was time to discard our army fatigues and all discernible military wear in order to easily mingle with the masses.

We will have to remain mobile in all situations in Assam. I get everyone together. 'Dear co-fighters. This may be our last day in Bhutan. We will have to decide our future course of action. We will have to take the common people into confidence. We will not look back. Many will think we are finished. Revolutionary moments are as trying as this. We should not lose hope. In fact, before 15 August 1947, when the Indians were under British rule, thousands of freedom fighters had to lay down their lives. I will not say that everything will be possible, but none of us should betray the common man or the ideals of the organization. Every life is dear to us. If anyone asks about Bhutan, tell them about the poverty, hardships and simplicity of the people of Bhutan. Talk about their hospitality. The Assamese people should not forget the Bhutan king's betrayal in another 1000 years. Try to avoid the enemy and penetrate inside. If unavoidable, fight back at storm's speed. The first three escorts can fire at will. The ones who flee will be shot.' When nobody had anything to say, we embarked on our journey again.

Page 35

It is no longer possible to stay together. At night, foot patrolling by the security forces takes place. Now getting caught means a dent in the struggle. We have lost touch with our organization. And the enemy's rumours might affect the mentality of our cadres and might deter them from their path.

I called our NDFB brother and explained everything to him. He was heartbroken. He was a simple boy and had joined the outfit right after his high school. He was from an interior village in Dhubri and knew nothing about the outside world. We explained the route to him and gave him Rs 3000. I told him that I would inform his official if I met them. His advantage was that his name was not included in the enemy list. When we finally took leave, he became emotional and started crying. Our eyes too became moist.

Page 36

Hiding in the forest, we kept an eye on the villages. Woodcutters and cowherds started coming in groups. As soon as it was dark, we proceeded to the village carefully. We entered a house and identified ourselves. The man had little knowledge of the outside world. Taking two boys with us, we went to the neighbouring village (inhabited by Nepalese people). The information helped us. We were relieved. The night would pass off easily and we would reach a comfortable place. The lady of the house gave us food and we regained some strength. We started walking. New camps were being set up by the army.

We entered a village and soon the whole village came to know about our presence. They wanted to know what had happened in Bhutan. The crowd sympathized with us; some were very angry and spoke of revenge. We felt good that these were our own people, for whom we were struggling. We pledged to fight till the last.

Page 37

We met the crowd and promised to meet again. It was time to leave. We started crying thinking of the lost ones. Among the ones who survived, nobody wanted to die. We parted ways and promised to meet again. But deep in our hearts we knew that such promises are often futile. I went ahead towards the river. Everyone got down at the shallow river and started walking. The dogs were barking. Everything was quiet. The evening stars were dancing in the sky. My heart could only hear the 'tup-tup' sound of the water.

~

On 20 August 2012, Guwahati city police arrested Hira Sarania.

5

THE SNIPER

In Assamese and the Bodo language, the word 'sila' means 'kite'. In Bodo language, *'sila megon'* means possessing eyes like a kite's. Anybody with sharp eyesight is compared to that of a kite's. Clad in a T-shirt, trousers and a pair of military boots, he grabs a plastic chair near me. He is accompanied by four other cadres. I gawk at him. I have never met a sniper before! A senior member of the militant outfit National Democratic Front of Bodoland (NDFB), Sila is a ruthless sharpshooter who is widely known for his nimbleness, and who, like a kite, never misses his target.

However, unlike his name, Sila looks unassuming and shy. A wiry man of medium height and wheatish complexion, he sits quietly and patiently answers my questions. I ask him about his life, childhood, hopes, aspirations, violence, prejudices and guns. He veers away from personal questions and talks about his organization. There is substance to Sila that I cannot miss. Many thoughts come during the interaction and I pen them down for future use. I can feel him dropping his defences and getting comfortable with his narration. The earthy timbre, the abandon and his passion for his 'cause' is undeniable. Not even for a moment does he look into my eyes. Maybe it's out of respect for women. However, I can also sense that he is perceptive.

He seems to have the right mix of assertiveness and reserve. Sila's replies become less forthright when I ask him pointed questions about NDFB—its past, present and future. After a while, I see him growing impatient. Probably, I have touched a nerve. He abruptly stops and smiles. 'You are asking so many questions. Are you an agent of the government?'

I burst out laughing.

It did not occur to me that a curious journalist's questions would evoke such a reaction. I am numb for a moment. I tell him, 'No, I am not. What on earth made you think that I am one?'

He gives a wry smile. 'I know you are. Otherwise you would not be asking so many questions.'

I gape at him. As a journalist, I am used to asking all kinds of questions. But I also realize that reporting conflict is like walking a tightrope. Journalists have to face the wrath of both the state and non-state actors. Ironically, I can understand his anxiety too. Sila's life, in one sense, has been of a singular nature, and he is not used to being probed. As a dedicated member of the outfit, he led a 'free' life in the jungles. Usually, militants have a strong sense of alienation and a feeling that they have been wronged. They take up guns to set things right. Now after the ceasefire agreement with the Government of India, Sila the sharpshooter is 'stranded' at the 'designated camp' at Khumguri village in Assam's Kokrajhar district—waiting patiently for peace talks and a political resolution of issues. He gets up and disappears into one of the rooms at the entrance.

My trip to Khumguri is arduous and long. After a train journey and a road trip along lush paddy fields, I land at their designated camp amidst the serene precincts of Khumguri village. It is a memorable moment. I am surprised to see a small zoo inside the camp! In an area covered by barbed wire, I see, in small cages of wooden frame and net, rabbits, monkeys and even peacocks. I can see small deer roaming around the fenced area. I ask a cadre, 'Why do you have so many animals here?'

He replies, 'We love animals. We want to care for them.'

I tell myself, 'But this is a mini-zoo!' By and large, the animals seem friendly and at peace, a setting at harmony with nature.

I am at the designated camp set up for the NDFB cadres who have declared ceasefire. Once branded the most dreaded militants in the north-east—treated on a par with the LTTE (Liberation Tiger Tamil Eelam) of Sri Lanka—they now lie low. On 25 May 2005, at New Delhi, the Government of India, Government of Assam and the NDFB signed a tripartite ceasefire agreement, according to which the NDFB cadres are supposed to stay in plots of land allotted by the government. The outfit was established on 3 October 1986, and initially set up as the Bodo Security Force (BdSF) under the leadership of Ranjan Daimary, alias D.R. Nabla. On 25 November 1994, the BdSF rechristened itself as the NDFB. The NDFB was formed with the objective of securing a 'sovereign Bodoland' in the areas north of the River Brahmaputra. The NDFB has three battalions— the first battalion operated in lower Assam from Barpeta to Udalguri; the second battalion in Kokrajhar, Dhubri, Chirang and Bongaigaon districts; and the third battalion operated in Karbi Anglong district. I am visiting them in 2006, a year after the ceasefire agreement was signed.

It is a warm, sunny day, and I am sitting in a chair in one of the corridors of the sombre-looking camp, which looks more like a makeshift college hostel. The structure has bamboo-netted walls and is neatly coloured in green. The windows are mostly wooden. Pigeons, with squeaky wings, perched in a neem tree in the courtyard, are constantly cooing. I can see a few uniformed cadres troop in. Suddenly, the silence is broken with a loud chuckle: the sight of a man chasing a drove of piglets across the open courtyard. The man has a typical Bodo scarf known as *aronnai* tied around his forehead. He is wearing camouflage-patterned trousers and a black vest. He abruptly stops as he sees me, and his smiling face transforms into a solemn look. I wave at him and ask, 'What is your name?'

The young handsome man stops, trying to catch his breath, very respectfully folds his hands and utters the Bodo greeting. '*Khulumbai* . . . Laxman Narzary.' He then rushes off. Apparently, it is against the protocol of the outfit for him, a lower-rung cadre, to talk to a visitor without permission.

Laxman follows the pigs. I get up from the chair, take long, swift strides and follow him to the pig sty—a partly-open enclosure covered with used wooden planks. A few tin sheets are placed on one part of the sty for shade. The grey-coloured pigs with their piglets were covered with mud and are trying to grab a bite from two large aluminium bowls. Laxman and his associate, who is dressed in army fatigues and sturdy military boots, are busy feeding the pigs. They both seem to be happy to be in charge of the pigs in their new abode, the designated camp of their outfit.

However, I can feel an invisible wall around them. Most conversations are, in fact, left hanging in thin air. I am amused how the public relation officers (PROs) intervene and take charge of all parleys. Seeing my interest in Laxman, B. Rakhaw, the public relations officer of the second battalion, who is accompanying me, tells me more about him. I listen, fascinated. It's almost been four years since Laxman joined the outfit, and he has a lot of enthusiasm for the cause—liberation of his land and people. He has bravely endured every task assigned to him in the harsh jungles before cessation of hostilities. Now, he has been assigned the duty of looking after the pig sty. Coming from a farmer's family, he is used to these chores.

In his long innings of twenty years in the NDFB, Rakhaw has carved a niche for himself for his tactical acumen, and oratory and organizational skills. The plain vulnerability of life must have caught up with him. He is waiting for the day the government will invite them for peace talks before the ceasefire expires. Like most militant leaders, life started with a lot of idealism. Rakhaw's self-

awareness seems uncluttered. He shows different modes of
acceptance and denial. A science graduate from Kokrajhar
College, Rakhaw had earlier worked as a teacher without
pay at a village school. As a young man, he wanted to
change the society. College was a learning ground where
he picked up nuances of social, political and economic
life of the Bodo community. He was drawn towards the
struggle waged by the NDFB to revive the glorious past of
the Bodo people.

I ask him, 'Don't you have plans to retire?'

He is taken aback by my question. After a brief moment
of silence, he tells me haltingly, 'I too want to lead a regular
life and have a family. I want to come back to normal life.'

It is almost noon and I walk around to have a good look
at the camp. Everything seems quiet and self-contained in
the designated camp. At a glance, the camp looks like an
army barrack with six security outposts at each corner of
the boundary wall. But from inside it looks somewhat like
a dormitory with a long corridor. Built like a typical tribal
house, the walls made of bamboo mats are richly painted
in various hues. I am surprised to see expensive cars parked
at a corner.

I am curious to know about life in the designated camp.
One of the PROs is ready with his answers. I realize that
their entire media and publicity unit has been put at my
service. The PRO tells me about a typical day in the camp.
A day begins early at 3 a.m., which is followed by one hour
of physical training. The breakfast at 5 a.m. comprises
mostly rice, dal and sabzi, which are prepared by the cadres
themselves. Then, at 7.30 a.m., there is a roll call by the

camp commander. Breakfast is followed by helping the carpenter in his work (more rooms are being constructed to accommodate more cadres). I can see some of them tending to the garden and watering the plants. Everything looks disciplined and controlled. Later, during the day, the cadres keep themselves busy by playing volleyball, badminton or indoor games like carom. They have an early lunch at 11 a.m. and then they are free to read newspapers that come in Assamese, Bodo, English and Hindi. The camp, housing fifty cadres, has twenty rooms and one common room, a kitchen with three big stoves, a dining hall and a storeroom.

So many conversations in the real world exclude women. I scan my eyes to look for them. I can see some of them in the corridor trying to catch a glimpse of me. I wonder if women break new ground after joining a militant organization. Do they defy gender roles? Do they even aspire to? One of them ushers me to the kitchen. Their kitchen-cum-dining room is a long room with a desk and benches lined alongside the corners. Aluminium buckets serve as serving dishes. She introduces herself as Reena. She has a childlike innocence as she smiles and walks me through the kitchen. Her silver nose-pin stands out. The kitchen is brimming with activity and it is obvious that the women are in charge. Smartly dressed in army fatigues, they are preparing lunch for everyone, including me. I smile and ask them, 'What's cooking?'

'Rice, dal and chicken,' Reena answers. The others seem stubbornly silent. Their only response to everything I ask is a smile.

I can see a lady using a gas stove to cook the 'special' meal for me. 'We use firewood, and the gas stove is only used in an emergency,' one of their PROs tells me. I can see a carton full of mineral water bottles. And they seem to have brought their best cutlery and glasses out for me. A lady is washing dishes at the hand pump outside. A male cadre is helping her rinse the dishes from the huge aluminium bucket.

As I saunter around, the PRO catches up with me. He starts explaining again, 'We divide our work. Cooking is done on a rotation system and this skill is imparted to them during the training period.' Managing the day-to-day finances is another gruelling task. They depend on 'voluntary' contributions from the merchants and other well-wishers, which is allowed in the ceasefire agreement. 'The government wants all of us to be in the designated camp but they don't look at our capacity and resources,' he rues.

I can sense that a few female cadres are always around me. Maybe they were instructed to be there so that I feel comfortable. Just then, I had to go to the toilet. I gesture towards one of the women and tell her that I need to use the toilet. I am usually queasy about using the toilet at any odd location, though I always ask where the toilet is. I had initiated a movement called the Sanitation Scribes, a dedicated group of journalists across South Asia who write and talk about taboo topics like open defecation, menstruation and sanitary pads, and clean toilets in public places. One of the female cadres ushers me to the row of ten toilets. A motor pump has been fitted to the hand pump to collect water. I use the washroom that is remarkably clean.

It is afternoon now and I can sense an uneasy calm inside the camp. There is a buzz that of late some of their cadres were arrested and some killed. One of the PROs accompanying me rues, 'As per the ground rules of the ceasefire agreement, we can receive voluntary contributions as we have no source of income.' He insists that the NDFB cadres obey all the ground rules even when the government is harsh. 'We did not raise arms, though we have them. We are waiting on the dock and we want the government to invite us for talks.'

I feel one day is not enough to really delve deep into their lives. But then, it's difficult to get access to it too. I want to absorb as much as possible and turn to the female cadres standing near me and ask them about their attires. They tell me that the cadres have two sets of uniforms, and that they get to wear a civil dress for two days a week. The cadres keep vigil on the six checkpoints all round the camp. 'We believe in self-defence. And our recruitment is done on the basis of background, physical fitness and consent of the family,' adds Rakhaw. At 4.30 p.m., there is again a roll call and then the cadres indulge themselves in evening sports. They can go for prayer but it is not mandatory. The curtain falls on the day after they have had dinner at 7 p.m.

A cardinal principle of the camp is discipline. The cadres maintain strict discipline and are taught to respect their seniors. So much so that they do not even look a senior in the eye. Their Code of Conduct includes obeying orders; refraining from smoking, drinking or using intoxicating drugs; being polite and gentle in behaviour; and refraining from mingling with the opposite sex. Another code says that an unmarried member shall only marry after a minimum of five years' service, but he/she must complete twenty-eight and twenty-five years of his/her age. The constitution of the outfit states that every member of the NDFB shall be subject to disciplinary action as per rules and regulations of the Bodoland army formation for any misconduct or offence or violation of the Code of Conduct of the NDFB.

I can sense that the cadres are restive and apprehensive about their future. I meet a whole team of PROs. One of them almost wants to use me as their messenger. In his characteristic dry, crisp voice he repeats that they are waiting for negotiations. 'We have also asked the government to give us information about the whereabouts of our missing cadres, who were caught during [Bhutan's] Operation All Clear. Now a year has passed and we want the government to negotiate with us.'

The NDFB cadres, also known the Bodoland Army, with a strength of around 2000, dressed in army fatigues within the precincts of their designated camps are now leading a quiet life contrary to their wild, guerrilla-like existence they had led in the jungles. At present there are three designated camps— Sapkati in Udalguri district, Dhanbil in Baksa district and Khumguri (near Serfanguri) in Kokrajhar district. These designated camps house fifty cadres each. There are separate lodging facilities for the woman cadres and their families, which are scattered here and there.

Their life now revolves around activities like gardening, cooking, cleaning, animal husbandry, farming, and recreational activities like playing volleyball, football, carom, watching television and reading newspapers. B. Khaubla, a PRO, says, 'We have asked the government for seven designated camps to accommodate our approximately 2000 cadres, but only three have been allotted so far.'

But amidst this apparent serenity lies a sense of insecurity and apprehension which are visible in almost every cadre's eyes. They wait with bated breath to know what their future holds for them once the ceasefire expires. Will the government keep extending the ceasefire year after year? Will the government invite them for talks and help them back into the mainstream to lead a normal life? Or are they fated to go back to the harsh life in the jungles in the foothills of Myanmar, Bhutan and Bangladesh, or in different locations of Arunachal Pradesh and in the Garo Hills of Meghalaya, and continue their armed struggle to 'liberate their land and people'?

There are other developments that are disturbing for them. On 6 December 2003, 2641 cadres of the Bodo Liberation Tigers (BLT), another militant group of the area, renounced violence and surrendered along with arms and ammunition at Kokrajhar, marking an end to seven years of insurgency. On the following day, an interim twelve-member executive council of the Bodoland Territorial Council (BTC) was formed at Kokrajhar. The BLT, prior to its en masse surrender, had been observing a ceasefire with the government since 14 July 1999. This ceasefire was formally agreed to in March 2000 and, subsequently at the 20 January 2003 tripartite meeting, extended till 21 February 2003.

A tripartite settlement—signed by the Central government, the Assam state government and the militant group Bodo Liberation Tigers (BLT) chairman Hagrama Mohilary—led to the establishment of BTC. The settlement aims to end the fifteen years of armed struggle for a separate Bodo homeland and bring development to the long-neglected region. The memorandum of settlement will enable the Central government to directly intervene in the economic development of the Bodoland council, which comprises the four Assam districts of Kokrajhar, Chirang, Baksa and Udalguri. The settlement includes official recognition for the Bodo language in Devanagari script, the withdrawal of cases against militants, a Rs 500 crore aid package, and the establishment of a Central Institute of Technology.

I wait till late afternoon to interview Gobinda Basumatary, the general secretary of NDFB. As I am ushered in to meet him, I can sense that the other cadres are alert. Nobody looked him in the eye. It is time for serious talks. According to the Union home ministry's 1996–97 report, a total of 201 persons were killed in Assam between April 1996 and March 1997, 174 of which were attributed to the NDFB. Assam government released Gobinda Basumatary to open a channel of communication with the outfit's top leadership, reportedly based in Bangladesh. There had been many rounds of talks between the outfit's leadership and representatives of the Central government and Government of Assam in different parts of Assam and New Delhi. Finally, it ended with the signing of a tripartite ceasefire agreement on 25 May 2005, in New Delhi.

At first glance, there is nothing striking about Gobinda Basumatary. But he is wise while dealing with my questions. He is ready to talk to the government without the help of a mediator. He looks like one of those back-room strategy makers. 'A mediator or a group of mediators may not be necessary for us,' he says. He insists on a political resolution of their issues. He points out that his concept of a Bodo nation is different from the BLT's, as it is a historical claim. 'We were an independent kingdom even before the British came to India. We are demanding rights over our land as we had enjoyed earlier,' he says.

When I ask him about the possibility of forming a political party within the Constitution of India that serves the interests of the Bodo people, he is abrupt. 'This is a controversial question and I would not like to comment on it.' He explicitly states his charter of demands—liberation of the Bodo people and land. 'Our charter is ready and we are waiting for an official intimation from the government.'

An uneasy calm pervades the camp. I sense that the camp is restive and waiting for a solution, including Basumatary. He wants the talks to be held outside India. Till that time they had not received any emissary from the government. He is firm as he says, 'If the ceasefire is not extended and talks are also not held, we will have to pull back our troops and go back to our path of armed struggle.' He is determined and unequivocal while pressing for his organization's demands. The idea that dominates all the conversation is the political will of the Bodo people through negotiations. The Bodos are peace-loving people and they do not want to hear the sound of gunshots again. Everyone longs for peace to return to the area and the uncertainty to come to an end.

After some hard talk, it's tea time. I try to unscramble my mind as the female cadres come with a tray with cups of piping-hot tea and some biscuits. I once again contemplate the woman's life in a conflict zone: poverty, a largely single-parent household, poor security of life and property, restricted mobility, and limited livelihood options and education.

As I set off in my car, I stop a few kilometres away from the NDFB camp. I stop at a different world—a world where Bodo women have created beautiful weaves in a backdrop of violence and conflict. It is a world created by Malati Rani Narzary, a schoolteacher and dear friend, whom I lovingly call *baideo* (elder sister). A schoolteacher by profession, Malati baideo is a multitasker. 'You can also call me Multi. I do so many things,' she jokes. A sharp, typical whistling tune amidst the clatter of the handloom startles me as I step into the weaving centre. I step in its direction, and meet a beautiful lady dressed in a colourful *dokhona* (traditional attire worn by women of the Bodo tribe) who is winding up for the day. I ask her name. She looks shy. 'Sumitra . . . my name is Sumitra Narzary.'

Sumitra tells me about her life, which is not an easy one for a young unmarried girl from a village in Assam's Kokrajhar district. She has been waiting for a 'husband' while sitting idle at home. She used to tend to household chores and occasionally weave a dokhona in her grandmother's loom. She was tired of her dreary existence. Moreover, because of the constant bomb blasts and tensions, her mobility was restricted to some households in the neighbourhood. 'Sometimes, I felt like killing myself. It was almost as if my life had no meaning. It's difficult to be a spinster especially in a village. Everyone seems to pity you,' she says.

However, she is a different Sumitra now. She flashes a proud smile as she displays her new pair of gold earrings and set of cosmetics she has bought with her own earnings. 'It's a wonderful feeling, that I now have my own savings account and can buy things for myself. I can also contribute to family expenses. Sumitra smiles. Her life has not been the same after she got involved with Roje Eshansoli (literally: 'beloved weaving'). It's a cooperative society that trains women in improvised techniques in weaving and churning out contemporary designs from traditional material. Apart from weaving traditional dokhonas, she is also weaving dreams for herself. She is hoping to find a good husband. 'In fact, I will now be able to contribute to my marriage expenses also,' she says coyly. More than anything else, she enjoys the flexible working hours, where they have freedom to go home or even go fishing, her favourite pastime.

I hug Malati baideo as I meet her. Her spirit is indomitable. She is keen for these girls to learn to write their names and be able to keep basic monetary accounts. The cooperative society organizes training programmes on employment-generation activities like spinning, reeling, weaving of silk and cotton fabrics, and dyeing. Formed in 1996, Roje Eshansoli now has over 1000 women beneficiaries in Kokrajhar, Bongaigaon and Chirang districts. There are also several home weavers in remote and inaccessible areas. With the first step of weaving firmly in place, the second step of marketing their products followed. By overcoming the initial hitches, apart from being a hit in the local market, Roje Eshansoli now supplies their products to different parts of the world.

Roje Eshansoli is a succour to the women in the conflict-torn place. Malati baideo tells me that almost every Bodo woman knows how to weave. The cooperative society harnesses their inherent skill financially by marketing their products globally. She tells me how women are always the worst affected in any conflict. The Bodo work circuit, with high illiteracy, was restricted to seasonal agricultural activities and menial jobs. Malati baideo wanted to bring them out of this vicious cycle and help them lead a dignified life.

It is nearing dusk and I embark on my journey back home. The car is speeding on the road that leads to the highway. Suddenly, I hear my phone ring. It's somewhere inside my bag. It rings for a second time. I answer the call. The voice on the other end says, 'Baideo, I am Sila. Please stop wherever you are. I have something important to tell you.'

I tell him, 'But I am already late. And I am midway now. How can I stop?'

'Please listen to me. You have to stop.' And he hangs up.

I gather my wits. Why is Sila the sniper asking me to wait on this deserted road? For a moment, I feel I should just rush off. Then I feel maybe he is following me. I feel it is better to face him again. I try to put up a brave front. I tell my driver to keep going and stop at a place where there is some human habitation—village or a marketplace. After driving for a few kilometres, we arrive at a *haat* in a village. A weekly market seems to be going on, as I can see makeshift stalls. I get off the car and call Sila again. I tell him my location and wait for him. I wonder if he going to shoot me. Did I go wrong somewhere?

After waiting for almost half an hour, my patience is wearing out. I look at the time on my mobile phone. I feel I should be proceeding as it is getting late. Just then a big SUV screeches to a halt. I can see Sila and three others with him. Maybe they were his bodyguards. I tell myself, 'Does he need bodyguards?' Sila gets off the car and walks up to me. I am shaking like a leaf. But I keep calm. He is fidgety. As usual, he doesn't look me in the eye. Suddenly, he hands out an envelope and blurts out, 'This has my bio-data. Please read it.' I am aghast by this abrupt gesture. It is too unexpected. My hands tremble as I open the envelope. I can see a wad of currency notes. I am too shocked to react. He looks stiff and tries to leave in a jiffy. I call out, 'What is this, Sila?'

He humbly says, 'Baideo, this is for your dinner. We could not prepare dinner for you. We thought we might as well pay for your dinner.' I return the envelope.

'That's kind of you, Sila. But I don't need it. My office will pay for my dinner and travel.' He takes back the envelope and looks down. He stands still, avoiding eye contact. He looks embarrassed. I hurriedly sit in the car.

As the car drives off, I look back from the rear windshield. Sila is at the same spot. I can see him wiping his forehead with a handkerchief. He must be cursing himself. In the melee of the weekly market, he looks lost.

6

MISSION COBRA

I have a morbid fear of snakes, but have a few herpetologist friends. A wildlife activist friend from Margherita in upper Assam was known to rescue snakes that stray into human habitats. It so happened that one day he went to catch a monocled cobra that strayed into a villager's home and suddenly the lights went off. And then he committed a fatal mistake. He used his mobile phone to light up the area and catch the snake. The snake bit him. He died after his treatment got delayed by more than four hours. Often snake-bite victims cannot identify the snake, and doctors are unable to administer the appropriate antivenom. However, one herpetologist was bitten by a pit viper and it was probably the first case in the hospital when the victim could identify the snake and tell the doctors which anti-venom to administer. He survived.

As I set out on my own mission to meet the real-life 'King Cobra', I am a little anxious. Tucked into little pockets of my memory is my brush with people from the other side of the table—the non-state actors. There is no getting away from machismo stereotypes of people in a militant outfit. However, when one pursues them, their stories break many myths: At times they are intriguing and at times they are 'too ordinary'. Nevertheless, their stories shed light on a whole unexplained and unexplored world.

'Baideo!'

I hear a loud shriek. I am taken aback. I did not expect anybody to know me here. As I turn around, I see a peppy young lad barely out of his teens. I am rather tickled to see him standing near me, and his addressing me as 'Baideo' makes me comfortable. I was not expecting such a lean and skinny escort, and one so friendly. I cannot help smiling back.

Our conversation is interrupted by a phone call. The voice at the other end gives me directions—asks me to stop at the trijunction. He is one of my sources who has been helping me track the King Cobra. It is not really a secret location. I am now standing in a nondescript village square. I can see a mud track ahead and lush green forests at a distance. There are a few odd shops with bamboo walls covered with either thatched or silvery tin roofs. 'Sanjay Pan Shop'—hung a small red signboard outside a shop that displays colourful strips of pan masala, gutkha, potato chips and dried tamarind. Adjacent to it is a tea shop. I can see steam coming out of the blackened kettle placed on a kerosene stove. A middle-aged woman dressed in a faded green cotton sari, with her hair neatly tucked in a bun, is frying pakoras at a circular cooking pot in another stove.

I sit down in one of the benches laid out in front of the tea shop. The shop acts as a magnet for people to come and sit, sip a cup of tea and greasy fried snacks. Often these kinds of tea shops are the hub of news, gossip and heated debates. I can hear a loud roar of engine and a noisy, overloaded auto van screeching to a halt. Men, women and children clamour out of the van and disperse in different directions. One woman carries two chickens with their feet firmly tied with a rope. Some of the men go to nearby bushes to answer calls of nature. I can get the distinct smell of drying urine.

And lo! My man Friday. 'How are you?' he asks confidently in English, his face showing no anxiety. He grins and seems thrilled to see me. Maybe he is feeling elated that he is escorting a journalist to their camp. He seems more excited than I am. I strain my eyes to observe him closely. He looks like a high-school kid! Clad in an orange T-shirt, an inexpensive pair of sunglasses and a pair of fancy jeans with a slogan 'Love is life' embroidered on the knee, my escort sways like a film star. The smooth sound of the voice strikes me, and he chuckles, 'I am Rituraj. Rituraj Murmu. I have come to take you to our camp.' I am impressed by his flair for conversation and his 'English' words and sentences. In the tea gardens, smatterings of English, vestiges of a colonial time, are venerated and spoken with pride. Knowledge of English helps break many walls.

The outfit that Rituraj belongs to is inconsiderable compared to the other big ones. Over the years, north-east India has witnessed the growth of several militant outfits—some big and some ragtag. Adivasi Cobra

Military of Assam is one such small outfit operating mostly in lower Assam.

Suddenly, Rituraj looks around and squeals, 'Baideo, where is your TV camera?' I am taken aback. I explain that I work for a magazine and not a TV channel. He looks crestfallen. I assume he is dressed in his best attire because he thinks that he will appear on TV. He was probably expecting a bevy of cameras.

A while ago, I was on the road to Srirampur Gate, a check gate on the border of Assam and West Bengal. Meandering down a narrow bumpy road that turned left just before reaching Srirampur Gate, I see squalid Adivasi relief camps. The heterogeneous Adivasi community of lower Assam, comprising mainly Santhal, Oraon, Munda, Kharia, Shawra, Bhumij, Bhil and Ho tribes, has had to face the worst ever ethnic conflict with members of the Bodo tribe in 1996.

A red cap on his head shows Rituraj's rustic elan. He is on a motorcycle, the only viable mode of transport in the inaccessible terrains of Tungsi in lower Assam's Dhubri district. I embark on my journey to their hilltop headquarters at Tungsi, some 4 kilometres from the Bawnoi Dingding, a small river, which is traversed by a rickety bridge that can be crossed only on foot or a motorcycle. 'Hope I don't fall off. Do you know how to ride a motorcycle?' I ask Rituraj. However, the thrill of meeting King Cobra overwhelmed any other feeling, even fear.

Rituraj is garrulous. He hustles his way to his motorcycle and mounts it. 'Hop on, baideo. Don't worry, you will not fall.' He laughs. As I brace up for this rickety ride along a muddy path, I try to look around me.

I can see lines of makeshift houses with half-naked children squabbling outside. Rituraj explains, 'These are the relief camps where the victims of the ethnic clash between the Bodo tribe and the Adivasis are lodged.' There are over forty-five such camps. On 15 May 1996, riots broke out between members of the Bodo tribe and the Santhal community.[1] The villagers fled and were temporarily housed in the primary school in the locality. Invariably, in rural areas, schools also transform into institutions for relief and rehabilitation during natural disasters or conflict.

The atmosphere of fear and mistrust had sunk and spread, and a group of Adivasi youths decided to form the Adivasi Cobra Military of Assam on 7 July 1996. The riots continued till 1998 and the armed struggle started with cadre recruitment and training. Ten years after they first raised arms to protest killings, I walk into their camp. My hands at times turn cold, my face steels itself for confidence, my head reels with curiosity and questions—I am mentally prepared for this uncertain journey. My only friend in this journey is my escort, Rituraj Murmu!

I feel like I have known Rituraj for ages. He has an interesting lineage. He is a descendent of the heterogeneous group of people who get clubbed together as the tea tribes. His ancestors were brought as indentured labourers by the Britishers from states like Orissa, Bihar, Jharkhand and West Bengal to work in the tea gardens. They still live in squalid, well-demarcated labour lines within the tea estates as closed communities. He grew up with stories of exploitation in the tea estates. The imported labour was forced to work as bonded labourers in the tea gardens in subhuman conditions. Young and vibrant, Rituraj is rather too mature for his age. He tells me, 'You see, in the tea estates, the tea bushes are pruned at regular intervals. Similarly, the minds of the tea garden workers are also pruned, then by the colonial masters, and now by the management. We cannot seem to think of a life beyond the tea gardens.'

Over the years, education has touched a few lives in the tea estates. Some of Rituraj's neighbours and family have moved out of the employment of tea gardens and settled in government-owned fallow land, or unused tea-garden land near the tea estates. They are, at times, employed as casual labourers in the tea gardens, and can live an independent life of their own. This section of people is known as ex-tea-tribe community. Another section of the community migrated mostly to lower parts of Assam and established themselves as agricultural labourers. Some of them were also rehabilitated in forest villages with small plots of land.

In a way, Rituraj is reinventing himself by trying to do something worthwhile for his marginalized community which was exploited for ages. His cause is personal and heart-rending. A young recruit, he joined the outfit in 2005. He claims he is twenty-eight, but I am not convinced. I tell him, 'You look much younger.' He laughs. I ride pillion on his motorcycle to reach their headquarters which is on top of a hill criss-crossing several villages and mud tracks. He keeps talking to me.

'Tell me about yourself,' I ask.

'I have done training in heater repairing from the Industrial Training Institute after completing my class twelve. My father is a retired government servant.' In a contemplative mood, rather too mature for his age, he says, 'We want to do something for our community. In fact, many of my young friends are trying to do different things, to bring about a social change.'

My escort is revered by a lot in his community. People get off their bicycles when they see him. I want to stop on the way as we pass through the relief camps. A foul odour emanates from the relief camps on the premises of a government school, which is occupied by over 204 families.

We get off the motorcycle and walk to the makeshift houses. Some youths are playing carom. They greet Rituraj with respect, and also gawk at me. We cross a drain and enter the row of thatched houses. A lady with her two-year-old daughter is sitting outside in the sun. Her hut seems to be tattered and the poorest. I can see cracks on the mud wall. Her name is Ritamoni Munda. Her daughter Manorama has been running high fever for many days. 'I have no money to buy medicines. I am using a herbal paste on her forehead which I believe will pull down the fever,' she says. Scars of dislocation are still fresh in her mind. Before the conflict, she used to till her own land. Now, she is homeless. She tries to make a living selling wood she collects from the forest.

There are signs of a new generation having grown up in the relief camps. Sarojini Kisko, a resident of the Tungsi relief camp, squats in front of the open fireplace as she moves a ladle in the huge pot. 'I have started growing some maize and selling firewood because I have to fend for my

husband, who is ill, and six children.' Most of the inmates
of the relief camps complain that they want to go back to
their fields but do not feel secure. Probably, the most tragic
tale is that of thirty-seven-year-old Mondol Hemron,
lodged in the Habrubil relief camp, at Gossaigaon in
Kokrajhar district. 'My entire family was wiped out in the
riots, but they have only been recorded as missing. Families
like mine didn't get any kind of compensation or payment.'

It must be so painful to be displaced from one's own
hearth and home. Life moves on in its slow grind for the
displaced people at the camps. As days drag by, naked and
malnourished children play outside the cramped huts as
the elders worry about arranging the next meal. There is
no drinking water, no electricity and no medical facility.
Rituraj tells me that diseases like tuberculosis (TB) are
rampant in his area. He smirks. 'Many families have
perished due to TB. The government claims of eradicating
TB are a big farce.'

This is one India that is forever playing catch-up. I had
once, in 2008, come across the story of how families had
perished to TB in the tea gardens of Assam. I still remember
the frail and lanky thirteen-year-old Lakheswari Bhumij
who was grieving the demise of her elder brother Ganesh.
He had died of TB, an ailment that could have been cured
with freely available medication. It was after her father, a
daily-wage labourer who died of TB three years back that
her family members started contracting the disease—first
it was her mother, then her brother, and then she herself.
There was fear in her eyes. 'I have segregated my utensils,
and my bed clothes, and covered my sputum with soil.

Maybe the germs are still around in our compound,' she says despairingly.

The journey to meet King Cobra will be incomplete without the sorry tales of the tea garden workers—the lack of healthcare and education, rampant alcoholism and the scourge of loan sharks.

We get on the motorcycle once again and I can see we are nearing the den of King Cobra. We were on the top of a hill. The red muddy track leading to the camp is bumpy. The blazing July sun seems to cut through the cagey-looking young cadres who surprisingly stand guard with bow and arrow. Rituraj stops his motorcycle and I try to shrug off dust from my kurta and fix my hair. I was not prepared for this turbulent ride on a motorcycle.

As we near the headquarters, the rider carrying my photographer cannot keep his balance and they both fall down on the muddy track, much to the amusement of some village lads thronging to have a glimpse of us. As I get down, I clutch my handbag and walk to the colourful tent erected in my honour! Tents are erected usually only to celebrate marriages or other happy occasions. Rows of plastic chairs have been lined up. The mood is celebratory. A young man dressed in army fatigue walks up to me. He introduces himself as Rimil Raj Kisko, the Secretary General of the outfit.

I try to feel the bow held by one of the cadres. Kisko dissuades me. 'The bow and the arrow that they hold are symbolic of many things—honour, pride and a traditional weapon to shield our community. The tip of the indigenously made arrow is dipped in cobra venom and red chilli powder while being hammered by the local Adivasi ironsmith.'

I gape at him, intrigued.

Kisko goes on, 'This nimble weapon is more effective as it makes no sound, and our opponents cannot make out who's shooting at them and from where. One can even climb on top of a tree and attack with great deftness.' By now, I am convinced that this bow and arrow combination is better than an AK-47.

I am ushered into the tent, and make myself comfortable on a plastic chair. The office-bearers come one by one and introduce themselves. The total strength of the outfit is 450 cadres with officials. I can sense a simmering discontent after I meet the chief organizing secretary of All Adivasi Students Association of Assam, Bosco Chermaco. Objectivity is often the first casualty of conflict. He says, 'We had to defend ourselves as the administration did not take an impartial stand during the riots. Moreover, we have to face frequent attacks by the other two Bodo militant groups, the now disbanded Bodo Liberation Tigers (BLT) and the National Democratic Front of Bodoland (NDFB).'

Finally, I am with the Cobras—not one but a whole lot of them. I cannot resist asking them about the strange yet striking name of their organization. Chermaco says, 'We decided to call ourselves "cobra" as we wanted to have an extraordinary name.' They also have a kind of logo or a symbol—a cobra and a bow and arrow. Metaphorically, these angry youths are cobras spewing venom on their 'opponents'. The outfit has been operating with their traditional weapons even after acquiring modern sophisticated weapons like

LMG, carbine, SLR (self-loading rifle), grenades, AK-47, .303 rifle and small arms like pistols, etc.

Kisko, however, denies any kind of links with other militant outfits like the Kamtapur Liberation Organization (KLO). He proudly claims how well trained their cadres are. They are trained in the dense forest areas of Shikhargarh in Kokrajhar district by ex-army personnel from their own community. And they are now dependent on contributions of their well-wishers. The outfit, which is under ceasefire now, vows not to rest till they fulfil two of their main demands—Scheduled Tribe (ST) status for their community and rehabilitation of their people who are languishing in the various relief camps set up by the government.

The cadres must abide by outfit rules. Cadres have to have passed class eight, and are banned from consuming liquor and marrying. There is a provision for retirement after five years of continuous service.

I turn towards another young cadre. John Barlo, twenty-six, is an undergraduate and hails from the neighbouring Morenai Tea Estate where his father is an employee. He joined the outfit in August 1996. Brandishing his bow and arrow, he says, 'Our people were being killed and my family comprising my parents, two elder brothers and one sister encouraged me to join the outfit. We had to take the risk as our aim was a return to a normal life.'

As I step into a makeshift tent, the unassuming and soft-spoken chairman of the Cobra Military, thirty-four-year-old Xabrius Khakha, steps forward to greet me. He is a little awkward; I did not quite understand the reason why. He has a fascinating background. After completing his class twelve, he had taken religious education (Roman Catholic) from Tezpur Mukti Data seminary in Sonitpur district of Assam. The priest-turned–militant leader Xabrius Khakha is remarkably gentle, his voice velvety with a subtle power. Clad in white shirt and grey trousers, he has more salt than pepper in his hair. He speaks at length on how he stepped out of his ordained profession to form the outfit and what he hopes to achieve from it. Waiting in the wings were a group of young cadres in their army fatigue. One of their commanders gave out a loud cry and they marched past me in a parade, showcasing their weapons, an honour reserved for heads of state in our country! I was overwhelmed by this rare honour— that too for a journalist!

Khakha leads me to a table with a few chairs. We sit facing each other along with some other members of his outfit. He isn't spontaneous. Khakha plainly explains the tricky issues confronting his community. 'Unlike other militant groups, our goal is different. We were compelled to form this organization as we saw our people being killed and harassed in front of our own eyes. In fact, we are now a formidable force.'

His arguments are banal and flat-footed. But he knows that his cadres are watching him. He is their hero.

'When Shibu Soren can be an ST in Jharkhand, why can't a Soren in Assam get the same status? We are clubbed together as a tea-tribe community, though we are in no way connected with tea here. But here we have been cultivating rice for the past so many years.' Khakha must have sensed the dire burden of consequences piling up at his door. He shrugs and smiles. 'I agree. Forming a political party and using a more democratic means to achieve our goals will be more fruitful. We may resort to such means later. We have highlighted our problems to the political leaders in Jharkhand to take up the issue of granting us ST status. They have reacted positively to our problems.'

He wants accountability and transparency to the funds spent and asserts that everyone should benefit from equal opportunities. He wants tripartite talks with the Central as well as the state government.

I have an inchoate idea of what it means to be an Adivasi. Sitting with Khakha, I recalled a shocking incident that took place in broad daylight in the streets of Guwahati city, just a few kilometres away from the state assembly in the year 2007. Lakshmi Orang, a twenty-five-year-old girl from Japaubari in Biswanath Chariali in Sonitpur district, who came to Guwahati city on 24 October for the first time to participate in a rally, would leave it mutilated and scarred for life. Organized by the All Adivasi Students' Association of Assam (AASAA) to demand ST status for their community, the peaceful rally soon turned violent. Lakshmi was shocked when a group of youths stripped her and as she scurried for cover, they ran after her and gleefully clicked her picture with their mobile phones and cameras. Later, while recovering from the shock in her home in Biswanath Chariali, she remained oblivious to the fact that the haunting shot of her being stripped was being flashed by television channels all over the country. This young girl did not realize that her maiden trip to Guwahati would spark off another agitation against atrocities on the weak and the oppressed.

My conversation with Khakha is nearing an end. I check the time. It's almost 3 p.m. I can see hectic activity on the other side of the tent. I can smell firewood burning. I realize something is 'cooking'. I get up, ready to leave. Khakha immediately stops me. 'We have made special lunch for you. You must have lunch with us.' I have encountered heartfelt hospitality whenever I have visited militant camps in the remotest of places. It is late afternoon and I have to rush back. I apologize and tell him I have to leave before it is dark. Khakha looks upset as his team had made elaborate arrangements for me.

As he shakes my hands and bids me goodbye, he adds, 'We have promised two things to our community. If this simple demand is not met, we might have to go back to the jungles.'

I look at my watch, sagely nod and wave at him. I hurriedly get on Rituraj's motorcycle again. He is more comfortable now and is constantly talking while we are on our way back. He asserts, 'I have no links to my family. My status was elevated the moment I joined the outfit, as people from my community now treat me with respect. My other classmates are working for their personal gain, but I am ready to sacrifice my life for my community.'

I had met several such young people who have carved a niche for themselves, albeit on different paths. What can be the future of a community with a past that's shaky and a present that's even more frail? Does it lay in the hands of the younger generation like Rituraj? Why is it that young

kids like Rituraj do not bat an eyelid while holding an
AK-47? As we near our vehicle, I get off the motorcycle. I
have a packet of potato chips in my handbag. I take it out
and give it to Rituraj. He grabs a quick bite and gives an
unblemished smile. 'Thank you, baideo.'

As I cross a tea estate, I can hear a tea plucker sing a
plaintive song that narrates the blistering reality of the tea
garden workers of Assam.

Sardar bole kam kam,
Babu bole dhore aan,
Saheb bole libo pither cham
He bideshi shyam
Phaki diye anilo Assam

Sardar says work harder,
The superviser says catch them and bring them,
Saheb says I will strip your back.
These white-skinned foreigners
Deceived us and brought us to Assam.

7

MEDIA-SAVVY MILITANTS

The Think Tank

ULFA, late 1980s. Exciting things are happening in the publicity wing of the outfit. The fledging publicity wing is witnessing some major changes, with its foray into cyberspace, its first major brush with technology! In 1989, the banned outfit acquired its prized possession—an Apple Macintosh for a precipitous price of Rs 1.5 lakh from Dhaka, the capital of Bangladesh. It is a closely guarded secret and the then ULFA publicity secretary Sunil Nath, alias Siddhartha Phukan, is one of the few people who knew about it.

It is not a regular acquisition. It changed the way the outfit delivered messages in its early days. In the initial years, militant groups used human couriers (even women) to deliver messages. This system has its pitfalls—the danger of being caught by security forces. But the proliferation of the Internet changed things. Nath propelled the IT revolution in the outfit, creating a safe space, overcoming psychological and geographical barriers, for sending messages to the outside world, especially the media.

Nath is always gentle and solicitous. Fluent in English as well as Assamese, this former ULFA top gun has engaging stories to tell. There is never a boring moment with him. I have always found him invigorating and intellectually inclined. I have had long conversations with him, who was once one of the think tanks of the proscribed outfit. Media-savvy and a master narrator, he was literally the voice of the ULFA, and an effective voice. In a conflict situation, rumours fly thick and fast, which is why militant outfits were conscious of the power of the media to put across their views. Therefore, the publicity wing of an insurgent outfit was one of its most vital operations.

I patiently listen as we have a long conversation on ULFA supremo Paresh Baruah (PB). He tells me why PB has managed to elude the security forces for so many years. One of the basic tenets of guerrilla warfare is that 'the city is the cemetery of revolutionaries', and PB follows that principle unerringly. He generally avoids cities and prefers the jungles, unless, of course, when he is in a foreign country. He avoids all kinds of civilian contact, except telephonic conversations. Many people talk to him regularly but never get to meet him. Except for a few senior members of the outfit, he is just a name for many. He deliberately maintains his distance from everyone, as if they will be able to pre-empt his moves, if people get to know him.

PB has been on Assam Police's 'Most Wanted List' for many years now.[1] I find it intriguing that PB started writing regularly in the local language dailies. Nath explains that it is not the first time that he has written articles for the newspapers. He writes on and off whenever he feels he wants to write and express his views. It may not necessarily be that he is trying to reach out to the masses. Nath insists that Baruah is capable of writing and that nothing is ghostwritten. 'In fact, in his schooldays, PB used to get merit scholarships, though he academically studied only up to class twelve. When I left the outfit in 1991, he was an avid reader and deliberately tried to pick up speaking in English,' says Nath. He adds, 'I may not agree with what he has to say, but I will always support his unconditional right to express his views.'

As a journalist reporting from a conflict zone, I am always intrigued by the publicity wing of the militant outfits. I prod Nath about his views on media. He feels that both the state and the rebels try to influence and, if possible, coerce the media. Moreover, the sympathy among a section of the local media for the rebels, i.e., the 'our boys' syndrome, affects its objectivity and neutrality.

Nath was in charge of ULFA's publicity and naturally had interacted with the media closely. After leaving the outfit, it was more of an instinctive act than a well-thought move to be a media person. 'I tried my hand in business too but failed. Media is the only field where I feel comfortable and confident. It was a natural choice,' he says.

He manages to build a cocoon around him with his pen. He welcomes the media 'boom' in the region. The rise in the number of newspapers and channels has effectively eliminated the 'syndicate' of media barons. It has become a lot harder for some individual 'media baron' to influence and manipulate public opinion for their own interests. The grip of some newspapers during the pre-boom days has proved unhealthy in Assam. 'I don't think the increased quantity has necessarily affected quality. On the other hand, fresh talent has emerged. Increase in competition has effectively resulted in increased efficacy,' he says.

It's a fact that journalists in the region often face attacks. Nath is against any attack on media persons and feels that these killings should be severely dealt with, and the government should be made to take prompt and effective action against the culprits. The media persons, however, should also remember that 'journalism' and 'activism' are two different spheres of activity. A journalist should remain objective and neutral. He is free to express his personal opinions through his writing, but his reporting of events has to remain objective. He, however, does not disagree with the fact that militant groups attack the freedom of the press from time to time.

He does not agree with the term 'mainstream media'. He doesn't agree that 'north-east/Assam' is a 'side stream'. He admits that we will have to understand that this region is neither the political nor the economic hub of the country. Being peripherally situated, naturally, it gets less focus than other parts. Remote parts of Assam/north-east India get less focus/coverage in the local media, as they are centred around Guwahati. Though unfortunate, it happens everywhere and at every level.

However, he finds it very disgusting when certain media houses act as mouthpieces of insurgent groups. 'I think

I owe an explanation here. The media houses, posing as supporters of the rebels, do so, not because of their love for the rebel cause, but because of their projected image as anti-establishment gets them better circulation.' Sensational and irresponsible reporting make them 'popular', while they go on dishing out distorted news and half-truths. It is indeed a very sad state of affairs.

He started off as a novice while being at the helm of affairs in ULFA's publicity wing. They did not know even the ABC of media. They did not go to any media school, nor was there anyone to train them on the nuances of media operations. At a later stage, however, they tried to train the 'boys' working in the publicity wing. The main source of news for the publicity wing were newspapers published from Assam, and some important ones from the rest of India and abroad. Radio was also a handy source, especially in the remote areas.

Nath doesn't quite agree that the pen is mightier than the sword. 'I believe both the pen and the sword have their own importance and relevance. I have always felt more empowered with a pen than a gun.'

Out of the ULFA, he is now relishing every moment of his new-found freedom as an independent media person. As a spokesperson for the ULFA, he spoke for organizations, espousing the official line, irrespective of his own personal opinion. It was more like PR work. Sometimes, he found it frustrating. But now he is free to air his own opinions.

Nath is used to fielding preconceived notions about ULFA and the sociopolitical problems facing Assam. He tries to focus more on the social problems through his regular columns in various newspapers, and his past association with the ULFA helps him in understanding their actions. 'I have tried to challenge some well-circulated "myths" regarding sociopolitical problems afflicting Assam, and I believe I have been successful, at least to some extent, in inducing fresh thoughts.'

The Editor

Mangaldoi, the headquarters of Assam's Darrang district, is a small yet vibrant city. I like its neatly paved streets and its bustling market. The road leading to his house is a typical narrow lane dotted with Assam-type houses on both sides. I drive down the lane that leads to his house. I stop when I hear the sound of a printing press. A small signboard at the iron gate says 'Saptahik Natun Prabah'. A room in his house is like a cottage industry that produces the weekly newspaper *Saptahik Natun Prabah*. It was founded on 19 October 2001. Its founder-editor Prabin Kumar Deka has an eventful past—he was the former assistant publicity secretary, Central Committee, ULFA.

His living room is spartan, with minimal furniture. As we sit down to talk over a cup of tea and thin-arrowroot biscuits, the floodgates of anguish and helplessness start cascading out of his heart. 'I was injured in an encounter with the Madras Regiment in a place called Senialpara in Mangaldoi. I was jailed under NSA [National Security Act] and TADA for a year. I was lodged in different jails—Mangaldoi District Jail, Tezpur Central Jail and then Guwahati Central Jail, and finally back to Mangaldoi

District Jail.' In April 1998, he was released on bail. However, it was a life-changing phase for him. He was at home with his injured right leg that was hit by a bullet. Due to lack of proper treatment, his leg's condition deteriorated leaving him disabled. Subsequently, he started limping. As he was disabled, he opted to take retirement from ULFA on health grounds in 1999. And, on 15 August 1999, he surrendered at the deputy commissioner's court, Mangaldoi.

He is in a state of drift as he tries to resume normal life. Like most militants who have spent years in the jungle, it is difficult to reopen the chapters of a regular life that includes paying bills, grocery shopping and fixing the broken windowpane. He tried to dabble in politics by contesting the assembly elections in the year 2000 as a candidate for the Asom Gana Sangram Parishad. He was even backed by the Asom Jatiyatabadi Yuba Chhatra Parishad. He was defeated.

Disappointments do not deter him. As he is trying to grapple with the grinding realities of life, his love for writing keeps him going. It is in those moments of despair that he decides to take up the pen to do something for the good of society. While he was in the banned outfit, he spent most of his time writing stories, poetry and drafting statements for the ULFA. He has a select group of friends. They encouraged him to revive his journalism skills and finally he took the plunge. He started *Saptahik Natun Prabah* from Mangaldoi under a group called Gana Sachetanata Prakalpa. The first issue was released at the Guwahati Press Club on 19 October 2001.

Most of his decisions in life are stirred by passion. His foray into the banned outfit is out of sheer commitment to a 'cause'—to work for the working class. As a postgraduate student of commerce in Gauhati University, he was also a committed member of the Students' Federation of India (SFI) in his hometown. Prior to SFI, he was with the All Assam Students Union (AASU). However, the middle-class politics disillusioned him. He rediscovered the passion for politics for the working class in the SFI. As a student, he read about the ULFA in the newspapers. He had read somewhere that the outfit was inspired by the Marxist ideology. In fact, he had read that once, during a raid in one of their camps, a copy of *Das Kapital* was found. This enthused him as a young student aspiring to give back to society. In 1990, he had also started working in the accounts department in a government office, but he resigned after he saw how inefficient candidates were being promoted. This young man had an overdrive of passion to do something for his motherland.

Thereafter, he took the plunge. After clearing the first year of his post-graduate course, he joined the ULFA in 1990. He was selected for training. Talented boys were attached to the political wing of the outfit. He was in the political wing and graduated quite fast—from being assistant organizing secretary of Darrang district to becoming the district publicity secretary in 1992. In 1996, he was made district general secretary, including publicity secretary of the district. By the end of 1996, he was appointed assistant publicity secretary of the Central Committee.

I am keen to know about his 'job of handling the media' in the outfit, though it was more of a PR job. He explains that his responsibility was to highlight the principles of the organization to the masses through their newsletters and statements. They had no specific training in the media as such, but they were given political lessons by top-rung leaders like Ashanta Baghphukan (who died during the Bhutan operation). As part of their training, they were told that the Russian Revolution was aided by some revolutionary newspapers like *Iskra* (Spark) that helped in publicity. *Iskra* was a political newspaper of the Russian Social Democratic Labour Party. *Iskra*'s motto was 'From a spark, a fire will flare up'. The French Revolution was inspired by the writings of Rousseau and Voltaire. Reaching out to the masses through the ULFA leaflets was a vital part of his job. It was important that the common people had faith in their outfit.

He sounds tired. He shows me the small room that has the printing press. I am the irrepressible journalist shooting questions at him. Deka is patient. He agrees that the pen is indeed mightier than the sword. He reiterates that the publicity wing was an important tool for an underground outfit. He smiles, 'A gun can be in the hands of a terrorist or a dacoit. If the gun can be a weapon, so also can publicity, organizing, diplomatic relations, and the pen.'

He tries to proofread a page as he talks to me. His new avatar as a media entrepreneur has not been easy. It is big money that rules the roost. Running a newspaper requires money and marketing skills, as a newspaper is also a product. He started off with 1000 annual subscriptions and he knows he can't really do business with his newspaper. He knows his limitations. He just doesn't have the knack for selling and he is expecting neither 'advertisements nor foreign investment'.

We talk about the terrain we both worked on, most often referred to as the 'periphery'. I can empathize with him. We both know the pitfalls of working as media professionals in the periphery, within great limitations. The region is marginalized, and there are not enough reporters. Media tycoons are not interested in reaching out to the masses in the remote areas. Most reporters lack a basic understanding of the issues of the common people here. At his own level, Deka is trying to talk about the common people and the problems at the grass roots through his newspaper.

An idealist at heart, he is a votary of the objectivity and reliability of newspapers; but these are rare. Newspapers thrive on the reliability of news. Deka points out that most newspapers don't bother to verify facts. They indulge in armchair journalism. Reporters are not paid adequately, and most reporters in remote areas and mofussil towns are either government servants or teachers, and one can't expect them to criticize government policies. Initially, Deka had seventy reporters from Darrang district. Now, 50 per cent of them have joined the vernacular dailies. At best, he was trying to create a platform for people interested in writing. 'We could not give them any remuneration, but saw the newspaper as a mouthpiece of the common people. We had mostly students and unemployed youth as reporters. We used to encourage them to write.'

In his stint at the ULFA, his team did intensive media analysis and scanned several newspapers. 'As per our analysis, some were in our favour, some took a middle path, and some sided with the government. No newspaper can be objective.' He feels that ULFA respects journalists. 'We firmly believe in the freedom of the press, and that the press is the fourth pillar of democracy. We know we should not attack a newspaper, and that is why we gave birth to our own newsletter *Freedom*. Our leaflets were very popular among the masses. We believed in giving an answer to the pen with the pen, and gun with the gun.' He feels that the media boom has led to more competition. It is becoming increasingly tough to survive in a competitive business environment. Therefore, media houses have to work harder to enhance quality.

He recalls his days in the ULFA without regrets. He feels that he is fortunate that he got a taste of the underground world, which is rare. These are experiences money cannot buy. He considers them a blessing as they have enhanced his analytical abilities. He had to come out as he was physically no longer capable. Sometimes, he felt that he had wasted the years spent with the ULFA. 'I feel so, as I have got nothing in return. My father was a poor farmer. I had six siblings. My brother, who was an SFI activist, boycotted exams; my younger brother was an AASU activist, and went underground during the Assam agitation. Both could not complete their studies. Maybe I would have been able to serve society better if I had taken up journalism earlier.'

I don't refuse a second cup of tea as Deka is sharing interesting anecdotes of his ULFA days, and I am relishing them. He recalls an incident on the occasion of Raising

Day (the day ULFA was founded, 7 April 1979) when he was asked to write a statement. Deka poured his heart out and in the statement he wrote that Pakistan could never be a better friend than India for the ULFA. Subsequently, one top ULFA leader called him and said he did not agree with his views. However, he got into a debate with him about how a fundamentalist country could never be an ally for their revolution.

Most media houses play a mind game. He agrees that some media houses exploit the sentiments of the common people in a bid to enhance their circulation. But they are all business houses, and do so only for commercial gain and not out of any genuine love for their country. They are not aiding any revolutionary group but only propagating their business by striking the right emotional chord. 'Some newspapers did support us—though tactfully.'

Deka lounges on the chair and stretches his injured leg. He has also heard that Paresh Baruah, the ULFA commander-in-chief, has started writing in newspapers. Deka smiles, 'Maybe he is trying to reach out to the masses, reiterate his love for his motherland. It could also be that he is using the media as a tool to justify his existence.'

As of now, Deka's existence revolves around his newspaper. A young boy walks in and tells him that he has visitors. 'Oh, they are some of my reporters,' he tells me. He had never imagined that he will be able to run his own newspaper. It's more than just a 'business' venture for him. It's his real-time connection with the society around him. It feels good to be back to his roots. 'When I first held my newspaper in my hands, I was dumbstruck. I was wondering whether it was a dream. I will never let this newspaper die, as it is not a commercial venture for me. It is very satisfying as I am in touch with the public now.'

Deka is an editor now, and he is proud of it. As an editor, it is difficult to be objective, but he has overcome it. As an independent editor, he enjoys the freedom of expression. As a person who has seen both sides of the conflict from close quarters, he can afford to be harsher in his criticism now. It is no longer a public-relations exercise for him. He can even criticize the ULFA.

The Idealist

As he tends to the pumpkin creeper in his small farm, he looks at peace with himself. He gently plucks the fresh green spinach, chillies and tomatoes, and places it in a bamboo basket. That's his lunch. He feels that if a man can grow his own food, he is the master of his soul. He stops to fix a bamboo fence with a sickle that was tied to a pole. It's a farm he has created for his sons. He feels that his investment in the farm is his savings for his son's future. He looks up at the sky to see if it will rain. Being a farmer is more of an intuitive and personal decision for him. 'I am the son of a farmer. I would have been a very good farmer had I not joined the ULFA.' I like the way he is seeing the world. He shuns laziness and believes that a community can progress only if they can imbibe a good work culture. My joy in life is to discover people with unwilted ideas.

This militant-turned-farmer-cum-journalist believes in hard work and is against running after easy money.

And yes, writing is Pranoy's first love. He enjoys reading books. He is a rare breed. It is difficult to imagine a militant enjoying poetry, stories and plays. Pranoy Roy had a literary bent of mind right from his schooldays. After he resigned from the ULFA in 1992, he decided that he would be happy with a second innings of life in journalism. He was the district publicity secretary of Goalpara district. Now, he is the district correspondent of local dailies published from Assam. 'I took up journalism as I wanted to keep the revolutionary spirit in my mind alive.'

After resigning from the ULFA in 1992, Pranoy started his revolutionary journey at the tender age of fifteen. He joined the outfit when he was in class ten in 1984. As a young man, he was emotionally charged after reading the leading writers of the period during the Assam agitation. He wanted to do something for his motherland. There were times when top leaders of the ULFA like Anup Chetia and Ashanta Baghphukan took refuge in his house and he interacted with them. They felt that he had the zeal and enthusiasm to be an asset for a revolutionary outfit like the ULFA. They encouraged him to join them.

Pranoy's father, apart from being a farmer and social worker, was the president of the village panchayat. When Pranoy told his family about his decision to join the ULFA, they tried to dissuade him. He hails from a big family— two brothers and six sisters in all. But he was determined. Nobody could stop this unswerving young man. He told them not to look for him and he would get in touch if possible. Otherwise he was leaving for good. His mother was emotional. But that was the time when there was mass euphoria about ULFA and many other youths were joining the outfit.

When he first joined the outfit, he was asked to fill a form and sign a bond never to leave it. The bond seemed to have come with an assurance that things just can't go wrong. As a young cadre, he had fire in his heart. Initially he was in the organizing wing and later the publicity secretary of Goalpara district. However, he became disillusioned with the workings of the outfit as there was no clear-cut policy on the indigenous population, or what the common people wanted. In July 1992, he, along with a few others, 'resigned' from the outfit over the differences between the top leaders Arabinda Rajkhowa and Paresh Baruah. Rajkhowa wanted peace talks with India, while Baruah disagreed. 'We wanted them to ask the common people of Assam what they wanted and work accordingly. But that never happened,' he said. Roy and his associates did not face any problem when they decided to quit the outfit. 'We did not bring back anything from the outfit. I even left my pair of shoes, watch and even the pen bought with ULFA's money,' he says with a tinge of pride.

Just as he is beginning to believe that he has made his escape, he realizes he is in a world he doesn't quite understand. He faces social ostracism now. During those days, Surrendered ULFAs (SULFAs) had earned a notoriety for their atrocities on the common people. He started living a secluded life. 'When we came out, people started looked down on us as SULFAs. I was uncomfortable. For one whole year, I stayed at home and read books.'

It is his indefatigable zeal to remain in reckoning that saved him from fading into oblivion. He insisted on sticking to journalism. In 1996, he started a news magazine titled *Bartaman*. It gained popularity and momentum but he could not sustain it due to financial constraints. He had even got a job as a tourist guide in the tourism department, but he quit as he felt he was not doing anything constructive. Moreover, he found it difficult to adjust to the work culture there. Subsequently, he, with two other youths (one of them a former ULFA cadre), started a local daily titled *Simanta Prahari*, where he was the news editor. It too closed down and then he joined another vernacular daily called *Natun Din* as its correspondent. This paper closed down. And from 2005 onwards, he has been working as the Goalpara district correspondent of a local daily newspaper.

His language is unadorned and blunt when he talks of his days with the ULFA. The sense of hierarchy and the strict guidelines and regulations stifled him. Often, their writings were censored. They also had a sense of power—the power of the gun. He worked diligently day and night. But he felt that he cannot work like a machine. His conscience troubled him, especially after the killing of Sanjoy Ghose, a pioneering rural development activist reported to have been killed by ULFA, and the culture of motorcycles and cars creeping into ULFA. 'But then we were made to write against our conscience at times. I felt it violated the basic ethos of why ULFA was set up in the first place,' he says. In a way, life was just as he was compensated with a life in journalism. Working as an independent journalist made him feel liberated and empowered.

Initially he had to endure the bad name of 'SULFA Journalist'. He knows he cannot afford to make mistakes now. He feels he has earned his credibility as an honest, fearless and independent journalist. He can even criticize the ULFA now.

The backbone of any militant outfit is publicity. He recalls his initial days in the outfit when he attended special training sessions. Eminent people gave them lessons on the ideological moorings of the outfit and how to maintain links with the public through media. He is sometimes overwhelmed by the present media boom. Now messages/information can be sent instantly. He feels sad when he sees many journalists compromising on their ethics and taking part in financial transactions. In many cases, the journalists have not been able to highlight the real issues and depend on speculations, which mislead the public. The national media too has not been able to highlight the region well enough.

A rebel has metamorphosed into a good citizen. He is now waging a quiet revolution with his pen against the injustices of society. His writing style is easy and effortless. He knows how to tell the stories of people and society without tricks and frills. He does not nurture huge ambitions of owning a car or a big house. In fact, in tune with his patriotic spirit, he has kept the surname 'Axomiya', meaning Assamese, in both his sons' names.

8

JUNGLE BOOK

He comes cycling down the rickety, muddy path from his nondescript village called Dhoba Ati Beloguri on the fringes of the 900 sq. km Kaziranga National Park in Assam. It is nearing noon. Golap Patgiri casts a furtive glance at us. He has reasons to be cautious, though. He has been accused of 'poaching' and has a number of cases pending against him, and has been facing the brunt of the Forest Department officials, who question him whenever any incident of poaching takes place.[1]

My car is parked near a *naamghar* (literally: 'prayer house'—an Assamese place for congregational worship, of the Ekasarana sect of Hinduism in particular), where I have tucked my three-year-old daughter, who is fast asleep at the back seat with my domestic help. I am leaning on the car, and wildlife activist Uttam Saikia, who is also the honorary wildlife warden of Golaghat district, is standing next to me. Golap's pace slows down as he nears us. I can see the tense lines on his forehead calm down when he sees Uttam standing with me.

Golap knows that I am coming to see him. Uttam has informed him. He smiles reluctantly at me. Golap then follows our car in his cycle towards his village. The road leading to his flood-affected village is in a deplorable state and the last stretch of a kilometre and a half, which has a broken rickety wooden bridge, can be traversed only on foot. I decide to park my car on the other end of the bridge, and tell my domestic help to take care of my daughter till I am back. I still shudder to think how I managed to cross the wooden bridge which had wide gaps in between. I had to take long strides and, in some parts, it seemed as if the bridge was falling apart. I screamed aloud when I narrowly missed a step.

His village looks sleepy. Assam's Kaziranga National Park, abode of the one-horned Asiatic rhinoceros and a UNESCO World Heritage Site, has been witnessing an onslaught of 'poachers'. When I heard another rhino was killed, in February 2008, I decided to investigate the problem personally. I decided to visit this nondescript underdeveloped hamlet which is infamously known as the 'Shikari Gaon' (village of hunters). I tracked Golap Patgiri, a man 'accused' of poaching,[2] who is now an activist and also an 'informer' for the wildlife NGOs and Forest Department. I realized that only people like Golap can give me a first-hand account of why innocent villagers end up assisting big-time poachers.

Almost in cinematic style, I encounter Holiram Patgiri, Golap's elder brother, who is an erstwhile CPI (ML) (Communist Party of India [Marxist-Leninist]) activist and a former teacher. He walks gingerly along the muddy track and was loudly singing a song. He has a booming and raucous voice. He is on his way back from Bokakhat town, the closest market around. My presence does not perturb him and he continues singing, about 'exploitation by the state'. He greets me. When his brother introduces me as a journalist, he stops and exclaims, 'A journalist?' He starts taking interest in me. He shows me an Assamese literary magazine *Prantik* that he has brought for his kids. 'I wanted to be a journalist too. It is a dream I could not fulfil. I wish my children fulfil it one day.'

As Golap quietly sits and listens, his once-activist brother takes a dig at the gritty realities of life, laughing. 'Can you believe it? We are citizens of an independent country. We are at just about 3 kilometres aerial distance from Bokakhat town, yet we have no electricity, no water supply or any government schemes here. The only saving grace is a primary school with one teacher to cater to 115 students.'

I get talking to him as he was more friendly, unlike his reticent brother Golap who would rather keep shut. I ask him how his village came to acquire the infamous epithet 'Shikari Gaon'? Holiram tells me that, earlier, the authorities used to grant gun licences to the villagers living close to the forest in order to protect themselves from wild animals. But later they were asked to surrender the guns after the militancy problem came to the fore. 'Many of the villagers had single and double-barrel rifles. In fact, land, elephants, buffaloes and guns were status symbols in our villages. My grandfather bought a gun for Rs 2500 and later sold it for Rs 7000.' Holiram adds, 'Most of our men were ace hunters, and hunting a pig or a hare was a sacred activity for us during our festivals. But the rhino was never our target. Our locality was a grazing area for buffalo, elephant and cow, and the gun was given to shoot in the air to protect them.'

As time passed, many of these poor villagers were lured into guiding and assisting the rhino smugglers and poachers who came from as far as Nagaland, Manipur, Arunachal Pradesh and Mizoram. These poachers come with sophisticated weapons, but they cannot operate without a guide who knows the 'ins and outs of the forest'. In fact, once fifteen such 'poachers' from the area had surrendered and the Forest Department had promised to pay them Rs 500 per month. But gradually the payment stopped, and the officers who came later did not bother. There were no proper rehabilitation packages for the reformed 'poachers', unlike for the surrendered militants.

During the tenure of Chief Minister Prafulla Mahanta, 160 casual workers from Kaziranga National Park and over 600 from other places in Assam were fired without being provided any alternative means of livelihood. Golap Patgiri was one of them. He worked as a casual worker at the park for ten years at a monthly salary of Rs 1500. He and many young men of his village and adjoining areas were rendered jobless and had even approached the Gauhati High Court pleading rehabilitation measures and reinstatement of jobs, but went unheard. 'We used to do everything from patrolling to cutting grass, assisting the permanent staff in almost everything. I had once caught a poacher red-handed,' says Golap. He narrates how he had once struggled day and night, sometimes without eating anything, to track and catch a 'pit poacher' (who digs pits to trap wild animals).

Everyone who knew Golap (literally: 'rose') as a boy remembers a quiet, solitary child—polite, affectionate— always outside in the fields and jungles nearby. He had several pets—from a wild turkey to squirrels. Rendered jobless after 10–15 years of service, these workers, including Golap, were affected not only economically but also mentally. Golap remembers one of his 'jobless' colleagues who lost his mental balance. 'It became very difficult for us as we were committed workers and all of a sudden we had nothing to do and a family to look after. It was difficult to come back and start farming in the village. As it is, the village is ravaged by annual floods and crops destroyed by stray rhinos and buffaloes,' rues Golap, who studied up to class ten. Hailing from one of the village's affluent families, nobody was even ready to engage him as a daily-wage labourer. He smirks, 'Instead, people used to ask us if we had a job for them.'

Holiram, who was listening quietly, starts getting edgy. He stands up and points out angrily that the Forest Department now claims that they are short-staffed and cannot deal with 'poachers' effectively. He thunders, 'If they are understaffed, why did they fire those casual workers? And our boys are brave, as they grew up among the wild animals in the forest. They can be better guards as they are not scared. Most of the present guards are of 50–60 years of age, who can barely hear, see or walk. How can they protect our rhinos?' His voice is so loud that a group

of children playing nearby look at him and run away. He
bellows again, 'And the weapons they use are so outdated
that they [the weapons] will refuse to fire when necessary.'

People like Golap and Holiram grew up playing in the
jungles of Kaziranga. They are familiar with not only the
terrain but also the sights and sounds of the wild animals.
Wildlife NGOs often suggest the government to employ
the local youth interested in wildlife conservation as a
special anti-poaching force in national parks and wildlife
sanctuaries. Local youths are best suited to fight against
poaching and other illegal activities.

Once a 'committed' forest worker, Golap was forced by
circumstances to assist the 'poachers'. 'It was a do-or-die
situation for me. I had to feed my family. I feel bad, but I
decide that I will go and come back with it or stay back.'
But Golap wants to come back to the mainstream and is
ready to surrender. It is becoming increasingly difficult for
him to travel for the court hearing as his financial position
is very weak. This year too his crop on his 4-bigha land has
been destroyed by wild animals, and he has to take care of
his wife and three children. He acts as an informer for the
wildlife NGOs and the forest officials.

Community participation is imperative for dealing with
'poaching' in Kaziranga. The government should accord
highest priority in strengthening the intelligence to stop
this second-largest illegal wildlife trade. Better protection
efforts during these years had led to an increase in rhino
population in Kaziranga from about 1550 in 1999 to 1850
in 2006. Unfortunately, rhino poaching incidents continue
in and around Kaziranga.

Golap is now a conservationist. He actively assists the young boys of the village with their NGO, Dagrob—Ecotourism and Eco-development Society. *Dagrob* means the 'to rise', and Golap and his villagers want to make a new beginning. One of their main aims is to create awareness about poaching and economically empower women through weaving, for which they are assisted by another NGO. Golap is hopeful as an NGO has promised to build him a shop, so that he can earn a livelihood.

Assam is not just a ground for human conflict, but interestingly also man–animal conflict. I remember how an unofficial curfew descended in and around Numaligarh Refinery Ltd (NRL) in Assam's Golaghat district as evening set in. Anxious shopkeepers shut their businesses by 6–7 p.m., as silence engulfed the area. Local people waged a daily battle as they hoped and prayed that 'baba' would not create havoc again.

'Baba' was what the local people called elephants. The local people worshipped the elephant, but they were also gripped by their fear of it. Marauding herds of elephants came all of a sudden, ransacked property and even killed people. Elephants were on the rampage in the state as human settlements had encroached on their habitat. The conflict had intensified over the years in Golaghat district and the local people attributed it to the setting up of the refinery at a location that was the breeding ground for elephants. The area was also a part of the state's largest elephant corridor.

Since 1996, when work on the refinery began, seventy-two people and forty-four elephants had been killed. The refinery was commissioned in October 2000 and was situated in the eastern end of the Kaziranga–Karbi Anglong elephant corridor, which had more than 1600 elephants. Wildlife activists said that this was the area where elephants used to drink water from the River Dhansiri.

I spoke to Sukhni Khujur, a tea garden labourer, whose twelve-year-old son, Gopal, was trampled by an elephant in November 2005 in Dholaguri Tea Estate. His widow Nirupama Khujur and three-year-old daughter, Dipika, looking on, Khujur told me, 'It was early morning when people came to wake me up. I did not have the faintest idea when he woke up and joined the crowd of elephant chasers. I had started shaking when I heard the news.'

Various news reports confirm the huge illegal demand for the rhino horn in East and South East Asia. The Convention on the International Trade of Endangered Species (CITES) states that there is a need for greater coordination among member countries to reduce demand for illegal wildlife products like rhino horn, which is believed wrongly to be a miracle cure in countries like Vietnam.

My second tryst with 'poachers' was in February 2008, when sixty-one poachers at Manas Wildlife Sanctuary surrendered and became 'reformed poachers'. Another UNESCO World Heritage Site, it was a tiger reserve, an elephant reserve and a biosphere reserve all rolled into one. Indian Forest Service officer Anindya Swargowary headed the Manas Tiger Reserve, and I had the chance to meet some of these surrendered poachers.

As I entered the sanctuary, I could see that Swargowary had arranged for interaction with reformed poachers, and there were a bench and a desk for me to sit. It was a classroom and I was sitting facing a group of 'poachers'. The meeting began and one of them felicitated me with a gamocha.

The poachers kept gawking at me. Some of them looked indifferent and some awestruck. I was particularly struck by a man sitting at a corner. He stood out for his thick, handsome moustache, almost like the sandalwood forest brigand Veerappan's. In a pleasant coincidence, this ex-poacher Dilli Boro was, in fact, popularly known as Veerappan. He smiled as he twirled his moustache. He was one of the most agile poachers in and around Manas Wildlife Sanctuary.

He was rather short-statured but his feet looked spry. 'Poaching is a gruelling task.' He smiled. Armed with a rudimentary country-made gun, thirty-year-old Dilli was at home in the jungle. He knew each and every nook, brook and hill of the rough terrain, so much so that he could differentiate the smell of each and every animal. While I nibble on a salted biscuit and a steaming cup of tea, Dilli told me the basic make-up of a good poacher: 'an understanding of the laws of the jungle'. That entailed sensing animal movement, swimming, crawling and even climbing trees. A good poacher should know the proportion of gunpowder to use and the number of pellets to be fired. Confident of his skills, Dilli claimed he had never returned empty-handed from a poaching expedition.

As I was listening engrossed, my three-year-old daughter woke up and started crying. I had laid her to sleep in one of the benches. Our conversation was interrupted and I had to go up to her and pacify her. She reluctantly took a chocolate I had in my bag, and came and sat next to me. As a working mother, I was used to juggling work and family. Sometimes I had to take my kids along with me on my reporting assignments. My daughter looked scared when she saw Dilli, and clinged to me. Dilli smiled and took out a toffee from his pocket and offered it to my daughter. He cajoled her and took her on his lap, and we continued our conversation.

Animal sighting, he pointed out, was a very difficult and challenging task. Dilli described a simple way of sensing the wind movement used by poachers of his ilk—lighting a matchstick and then blowing it off. 'The direction of the thin smoke will indicate the wind direction and we avoided moving in that direction, so that the animal doesn't get a hint of human movement.'

'So, who is a real poacher?' I asked.

A reformed 'poacher', Mahendra Sil, who was sitting quietly all the while, blurted out, 'There is no such thing as a big poacher or a small poacher. Anyone who dares to go to the jungle is a poacher and our eyes are always on a big animal.'

Manas Wildlife Sanctuary was a haven for all the large terrestrial mammals—elephant, wild buffalo, Indian bison and the one-horned rhinoceros, which roamed free and wild in one area. It was a haven for poachers. I listened astounded as Dilli listed his big catches, which included hundreds of hog deer, wild bison, wild buffalo, a one-horned rhino and even a royal Bengal tiger, whose skin fetched him Rs 26,000! 'In fact, I was waiting, perched in a tree, to hunt a wild boar but I sighted the tiger who had come preying on the boar. I was greedy, as a big animal meant more money. There were two hunters—the tiger and myself. And one hunter had to die.' He laughed.

These hardened ex-poachers hailed from the sixty-one fringe villages that were within a distance of 2 km from the southern boundary of the Manas Wildlife Sanctuary. These 'reformed' poachers were now committed to protect the same wildlife they had once killed. Anindya Swargowary, the forest official, had the foresight to understand the conditions of the people living in the fringe villages, and decided that 'conservation' and 'development' must go hand in hand. Most of these villagers were poor, landless labourers or marginal farmers with no other alternative sources of livelihood. There were no large townships or factory complexes, except a Fatimabad Tea Estate in Bansbari adjacent to the boundary. A major chunk of the population were from the Bodo tribe followed by other communities like Assamese, Bengali, Nepalese and some Adivasis. And the constant violent incidents caused by the militant groups further deteriorated their condition.

Swargowary enjoyed a remarkable rapport with the poachers. He managed to persuade them to come and join the mainstream and refrain from killing the animals. The authorities had devised this ingenious plan to protect the wildlife, divert people from poaching and give them alternative livelihoods. Sixty-one poachers who had surrendered before the authorities of the Bodoland Territorial Council (BTC) would now live and work in the jungle as members of the newly formed Kahitama Manas

Conservation and Ecotourism Society. Thaneswar Das, a reformed poacher, was determined not to allow his sons to step into his shoes.

What started off as occasional recreational hunting soon became rampant poaching within the park premises during the Bodo agitation of 1988–98. In 1992, UNESCO listed Manas as a 'World Heritage Site in danger' because of intrusions by militants, which caused a breakdown of infrastructure, looting of arms and ammunition and killing of staff, among other forms of damage and destruction. Manas, which was declared a tiger reserve in 1973, has suffered more loss of man and material than any other tiger reserve in the country.

The Bodo separatist movement had other repercussions too. It opened up the jungle for exploitation. With gun in hand, a bunch of unemployed youths started looking at the jungle for employment opportunities. Thaneswar recalled, 'We had practically no infrastructure, healthcare, educational facilities, water supply or irrigation. There was no avenue for work even as a daily-wage labourer. We had to feed our families.' Frustrated at being denied a job in the very forest he lived so close by, Das who studied till class ten had tried all options of obtaining an appropriate job before ending up as a poacher.

The indigenous poachers, who grew up in the jungles, devised ingenious ways to support each other and work together. They devised clever plans to hoodwink forest officials. The debutants learned from the veterans. For instance, they buried their guns in the forest itself, and to cover their tracks in sandy terrain, the last person in the group dragged a leafy branch behind them. Sometimes, they even drew tracks of tiger paws to mislead forest officials. Most of them operated barefoot. They also carried mosquito repellents, mosquito nets, essential medicines and painkillers, their own rations and drinking water.

It was a difficult vocation for most of them, as almost all of them were animal lovers. Anukul Chandra Das, from Kahitama Pathar village, said he used to chase away big animals as he used to hunt for only deer and wild boar, whose meat fetched him a decent sum. 'When there's no grain in your house to feed your family, you tend to lose all scruples and principles. I took to poaching only out of sheer desperation as all my crops were ravaged by deer, wild pigs and peacocks. I was anguished when I got a few sheaves of hay as compensation from the Forest Department when my house was destroyed by wild elephants. Once the Forest Department hired us as casual labourers but never bothered to pay us.'

Unfortunately, it is invariably the middlemen, also known as 'dadas' (literally: 'elder brothers'), usually from the 'town', who profit from the skin, horn, teeth and other body parts of these animals, which have a big demand in the global market and earn 'handsome' sums. Local poachers who risk their lives don't even know where to sell their wares or their real value in the clandestine global market, and end up getting a meagre amount. Also, if they accidentally kill a big animal, the body part or the skin might just rot or wither away if they fail to contact the middlemen. Sometimes poachers have to hire labourers to cut their catch, an expense that painfully eats into their earnings. For a big deer they had to give 4 kg, 1 kg for a small deer, and 20 kg for a buffalo to the militants (now under ceasefire).

Contrary to popular belief, poachers live in abject poverty. The story of Sipini Boro was heartbreaking. Her husband Naren Boro hunted hog deer for meat, but he could never take it home for his family. My heart skipped a beat when his coy wife said, 'I don't even know how deer meat tastes like!'

Almost all small-time poachers have a similar story to tell. Netra Bahadur Rai, twenty-six, who hails from the Nepalese community and has been poaching since age twelve, is very bitter. 'As a child I used to go to school, but I had no clothes to wear to school, or anything to eat after coming back from school. With poaching I at least got something to eat. If I had a choice, I too would have gone to school.'

Ranjit Boro of Chamtaibari, another fringe village, was rather embarrassed about his fame as a 'shikari'. He cringed as he spoke, 'I was a wealthy man with 25 bighas of land. But the River Manas eroded my land and now I have built a small house in the reserve forest.'

I walked away slowly. My job as a journalist was done. I have got my story. The next day, I sat on the banks of River Manas and tried to understand the glory of Manas where men and animals had coexisted for ages. In a bid to revive the old glory of Manas, the authorities had lain emphasis on community participation. The surrender of sixty-one poachers was a big step in this direction. As there were no concrete rehabilitation packages for poachers, the authorities were now planning to give them Rs 10,000 each, but in kind. Some will get a rickshaw, some GI (galvanized iron) sheet for roofing, and some with agricultural land will get a bullock cart.

9

REPORTING A FAKE ENCOUNTER

It is August 2009.

I walk towards the kitchen to check if the rice is cooked. I can see the rice cooker bubbling. I look out of the window. Everything is calm outside. A sparrow pecks on the glasspane of the sun-kissed kitchen window; the pumpkin creeper unfurls its stem and is trying to cling on to the bamboo pole for support. This is my favourite spot in the house, because I can have a peek at the vegetables growing in the yard. I am jolted back to reality by the loud pitch of the television anchor. I don't know what will happen next. I am unnerved and had not bargained for this reaction to an otherwise routine 'exclusive' story. Sitting on my couch in my living room in Guwahati, I am at an aerial distance of 269 km from Imphal, the capital of Manipur. On an ordinary day, I would not have considered this mammoth distance. But today, I am far from Manipur, yet I seem so close. News of a civil uprising in Manipur on

159

television makes my hair stand on end. An unknown fear grips me. Because, in a way, I am responsible for it.

On 8 August 2009, *Tehelka* magazine published my story titled 'Murder in plain sight', with a string of incriminating photographs shot by a local photographer. The story created a furore as it captured the 'encounter killing' of a young man on 23 July 2009. Mention 'fake encounter' and one conjures up images of secret conspiracies and shooting in some dark, lonely jungle road. But this shootout was even more unsettling. It took place barely 500 metres from the State Legislative Assembly, in Imphal, Manipur's capital, and in broad daylight. The twenty-seven-year-old Chungkham Sanjit, a former militant, was shot dead by the heavily armed Manipur Police Commandoes (MPC). Thokchom Rabina, a pregnant woman and a casual bystander, also died in the firing.

Richard Engel, in his book *And Then All Hell Broke Loose: Two Decades in the Middle East* writes, 'Reporters go through four stages in a war zone. In the first stage, you're Superman, invincible. In the second, you're aware that things are dangerous and you need to be careful. In the third, you conclude that math and probability are working against you. In the fourth, you know you're going to die because you've played the game too long.'

In many ways, I was progressing towards stage three. Some stories are life-altering. It is probably the first time that a 'fake encounter' has been caught on camera, step by step. The local photographer had feared for his life and chosen to remain anonymous, sending his photographs to me. At first glance, the photographs seemed too dangerous a story to publish. But I felt it was a truth that had to be told. And I was in a comparatively safer location, as I was based in a different state, and was not under the jurisdiction of Manipur Police. The story corroborated by the photos was published and it created an uproar.

It was the scoop of a lifetime. The story was picked up by almost all the media organizations of the world. One evening, as I was sipping tea, lost in thought, I got a call from a radio station in Toronto, Canada, and they wanted to interview me. Such was its impact that the story snowballed into a civil uprising in Manipur and life in the state came to a standstill for almost three months.

Yet, I felt nothing to be triumphant about. I was a lonely reporter in the neighbouring state of Assam. My story was just photographic proof of what many people already knew to be the ground realities, and an opportunity to vent their outrage against the government and the draconian Armed Forces (Special Powers) Act 1958. The Act, based on a 1942 British ordinance, to quell the Indian independence movement during the World War II, grants arbitrary powers to the armed forces to shoot to kill, arrest, conduct searches and demolish structures in the name of 'aiding civil power'. The powers that the AFSPA extends to the armed forces come into force once an area has been declared 'disturbed' by the state or Central government.

Ironically, this incident is not related to AFSPA. I write in the story:

In July 2004, the nation was rocked by the protests of a group of Manipuri women who marched to an

Assam Rifles base in Imphal, stripped naked and raised a searing banner: 'Indian Army rape us'. They were protesting the rape, torture and murder, a fortnight earlier, of Thangjam Manorama, 32, who was picked up from her home at night by the Assam Rifles. Manipur rose up in protest that day, and in August 2004, the Centre relented, withdrawing the AFSPA from Imphal's municipal zone. 'Post-Manorama', as history is marked in Manipur, the army has taken a backseat, withdrawing outside the municipality. In a seemingly, new counter-insurgency strategy, the Manipur Police Commandoes (MPC) has unleashed a reign of terror in the state. The MPC does not fall under the AFSPA but has now become notorious across the state. Extrajudicial killings, and, in particular, fake encounters by the MPC have become common in Manipur.[1]

As the uproar in Manipur continues, here I am waging a sequestered battle. The nights seem longer than usual. Images of the pregnant woman Rabina keep lighting up in my mind, as I try to go to sleep. It's unsettling and I have sleepless nights. It is also the time I am expecting my second child. One night, I feel uneasy and restless, and I am rushed to the hospital. My gynaecologist is perturbed by my fluctuating blood pressure, and rebukes me for not taking good care of my health. She had earlier warned me not to take unnecessary stress, to care for the unborn child. I start taking pills for hypertension.

As days pass, things cool down in Manipur. Life in Manipur limps back to normality. I start settling down.

Heavily pregnant, I am busy with my regular reporting and domestic chores. Meanwhile, the tortuous judicial proceedings begin and I am questioned by the special investigation team (SIT) of Manipur Police, the judicial commission and the Central Bureau of Investigation (CBI) in different settings. I start receiving veiled threats and realize the complexities of combat reporting. I realize, in this whole murky world of fake encounters and extrajudicial killings, I am merely a cog in the wheel. I remember a top police officer once telling me, 'Every encounter is a fake encounter!'

I am summoned to physically appear before the district and sessions judge, Manipur East. I refuse to travel to Manipur citing security reasons. In an unprecedented move, the judicial commission holds a special hearing for my deposition in Guwahati's Manipur Bhawan. In January 2015, on the day of the hearing, my hardy utility car wobbles, negotiating the traffic in Guwahati. I land in Manipur Bhawan. As soon as I park my car, I can see a minibus full of people stop there. I walk up to the two-storeyed building located in a residential area. A coat of paint and some repairs can make the building more appealing. I can see a wooden chair in a sitting area that seems like a lobby. I make myself comfortable. I realize I am the only woman around. The men who came in the minibus huddle at a corner. I can hear some mumbling and my name being called out in whispers.

I start chewing gum. One of them comes to me and says, 'Are you the journalist who broke the story of the fake encounter?'

I nod.

All of them look at me awestruck. He tells me, 'We are all journalists from Manipur. We have come to hear you depose. Do you know if you come to Manipur now, people will greet you with garlands and flowers?' One by one they walk up to me and shake my hand. I do not know whether I should be happy or worried. One of them looks concerned and is worried about my safety. He asks me, 'You look so young. Do you have children?' Yes, I do, I tell him. I try to hide my baby bump. I do not talk much as I am both tensed and cautious. I respond in monosyllables. I look at them and realize how important this story is for the people of Manipur. They huddle around me and tell me, 'Do you realize you have become a part of Manipur's history?' I look blankly. I just want to depose, go back home and have a steaming cup of tea to relieve my stress.

The deposition is harsh, but I come out of it unscathed. But I did feel like a criminal when the lawyer representing Manipur Police grilled me. I had the responsibility of protecting the identity of the 'anonymous' photographer. There is enormous pressure on me to reveal the identity of the photographer.

The legal proceedings are ceaseless. I was, however, relieved when the two-member special investigation team came from Manipur. They wanted to meet me in Guwahati, but told me that they will meet me at a place of my choice. I decide to meet them at the local police station. Then, came the summons from the CBI. I was asked to be present at the CBI office in Guwahati and a female officer was designated to question me. I had to struggle to climb up the stairs as my feet were swollen. My pregnancy was clearly visible. I was mentally and physically exhausted.

Then came the criminal case filed by the victim's mother. I am a crucial witness and I am summoned to the chief judicial magistrate's court in Guwahati. The court premises are busy as usual. I have never attended a court proceeding before. I wait outside the designated court of the judge who issued the summons. It's not a comfortable feeling. I sit all alone as a team of lawyers came from Manipur. They question me in front of the judge. The judge from Assam is clueless about the case and tries to read the pages in front of him. He looks at me baffled. The public prosecutor eyes me suspiciously. She peers at me and asks, 'Who are you? How are you connected to this case?' I seem like an unlikely witness for the case! The incident was investigated, and the police commandos who killed Sanjit have been charged; but, so far, no action has been taken against them. This is, however, not an isolated case. Manipur still mourns the extrajudicial killings over the years, and the relatives of the dead are yet to find justice. As I come out of the court, I see a group of young journalists with their television crew trying to grab an interview with a top militant leader who has been produced in the court.

The aftermath of my story is a sheaf of official summons that keep coming, even after a decade, making me relive that part of my life, again and again, when I had to appear like a criminal before the authorities. The impact of the story made me an insomniac. I had nightmares, and I became irritable, and started screaming at my child.

Nothing could make me happy. I started talking to myself. One day, when I hit my daughter over a petty matter, my husband decided that I needed counselling. We decided to see a psychiatrist. I was diagnosed with post-traumatic stress disorder (PTSD). I started taking antidepressants. The chronological sequence of my trauma makes for a huge learning experience in reporting conflict, which can spring and sprawl surprises on you at every step.

My friends organized a baby shower for me. But I was too sullen and dull to enjoy it. They seemed disappointed at my behaviour. I had to make an effort to smile and be part of the fun. Life seemed listless.

Probably, my experience would have been different if I had had some kind of support system. Unfortunately, there is none for a journalist in many parts of the world. When I discussed this with an Imphal-based journalist friend, when I told him that I am going through a traumatic time, his answer numbed me. 'Can you imagine our plight? We have to undergo this trauma everyday of our lives.' Manipur is among the most dangerous places in India for a journalist. Journalists have been subjected to all kind of atrocities: They have been killed, abducted, assaulted, arrested and media offices forced to close down. Sometimes, parcel bombs were sent as a warning.

There are certainly serious questions about the plight of a journalist reporting conflict that need to be addressed. What the camera and the story do not tell us is the trail of trauma that it leaves on the isolated journalist. I realize that nobody ever tries to delve into the life of the journalist who reports from a conflict zone. There is absolutely no support system to deal with physical dangers, legal rigmaroles and the psychological trauma that a journalist goes through.

A Hostile Environment and First-aid Training (HEFAT) is provided for journalists by the International Women's Media Foundation (IWMF), along with hands-on experience in reporting regions where safety can be an issue. I wish I had undergone such focused training. Our journalism schools are ill-equipped to train fledging media students on the nuances of conflict reporting before they embark on the field. I am a trained journalist from the Indian Institute of Mass Communication (IIMC), New Delhi. However, we were never told to take care of our own vulnerability and personal safety. I remember this conversation with a senior editor, who had extensively covered conflict in Kashmir. I told her, 'All these years of reporting conflict must have made you very strong.'

She replied, 'No, in fact, it has made me feel even more vulnerable.'

Haunted by the unsavoury experience of the past, I sometimes wonder when my role as a journalist ends. Where do I go after telling the story? Can I distance myself from the story? Do I have a say in the reconciliation process? Am I a part of the story? Or just a rank outsider? After all, I have also faced the trauma—psychological, legal, physical. I had attended a course on 'conflict transformation across cultures, peace-building training and education for SAARC emerging leaders' in Kathmandu, Nepal, in 2012. It was organized by SIT Graduate Institute, Vermont, USA. They spoke about reconciliation as an important part of conflict resolution. But I can see no resolution in sight. The transgressions continue. An activist friend aptly sums up the daily life in Manipur, 'Life in Manipur is like a lottery. You are alive because you are lucky.'

Reporting conflict keeps a journalist forever on the brink of peril. I try several times to write about my experiences, but it ends up as crumpled chits under the table. Many a time, we are not sure if we should talk about our weaknesses as it may affect our careers. I am forever looking for peace. As American photojournalist Lynsey Addario says, 'As a war correspondent and a mother, I've learnt to live in two different realities . . . but it's my choice. I choose to live in peace and witness war—to experience the worst in people but to remember the beauty.'[2]

(The case was finally transferred to the Central Bureau of Investigation [CBI] in 2010. And in a sensational revelation, one of the nine accused in the case, Thounaojam Herojit Singh, a thirty-five-year-old Manipur Police head constable and a gallantry award recipient, confessed to the killing.[3])

ACKNOWLEDGEMENTS

This book is my journey as a combat journalist. However, it is not my journey alone. It is the journey of countless journalists who work under tremendous duress in some of the most difficult terrains—geographical, political, social and cultural. I have walked many untrodden paths—criss-crossed broken roads on bullock carts, crossed streams on country boats and walked on precarious rickety bridges—in the nook and crannies of north-east India in the quest for its stories. Moreover, it is also the journey of the numerous journalists who have been reduced to mere statistics in the long list of killed, injured, abducted and jailed.

I had embarked on my journey within the safe confines of the editorial desk of *India Today* magazine at New Delhi. I got an opportunity to hone my skills with one of the finest copy editors, Joel Rai. Thereafter, I came back to report on north-east India. Most of my conflict reporting has been under the able guidance of another fine editor, Sankarshan Thakur. Of course, though I was on my own in the field, I am thankful to my numerous anonymous sources and contacts who helped me to get my stories.

As a first-generation journalist, my journey would have been incomplete without the silent support of my family (who sometimes were clueless as to what I was up to). My parents who supported my decision to be a journalist, though they had never met one. My brother who drove me to inaccessible places without asking any questions. My sister for being a mother to my two daughters when I was lost in work. My husband for being a constant pillar of support.

And then there have been friends and colleagues who have been immensely supportive. Thank you, Monideepa Choudhury, for suggesting the title *Bulletproof*. She told me, 'In many ways, you are bulletproof.' My heartfelt gratitude goes to Radhika Malladi, Sabreen Ahmed and Usha Raman for going through the drafts and giving valuable suggestions.

To Joseph Antony of Penguin Random House India for his meticulous editing of the manuscript. And to Premanka Goswami, senior commissioning editor at Penguin Random House India, for considering my story worth telling, and making *Bulletproof* a reality.

NOTES

Prologue

1. Sanjoy Hazarika, 'An abomination called AFSPA', *The Hindu*, 12 February 2013, https://bit.ly/2VANwzS
2. 'Safety of Women Journalists in Conflict Situations', The Permanent Missions of France, Greece and Lithuania to the United Nations, https://bit.ly/2qw8m40
3. 'Women journalists are attacked, harassed and threatened – in person and online – every day', International Women's Media Foundation, https://bit.ly/2EfVHeZ
4. Ibid.
5. Teresa Rehman, 'Who Is Ima Gyaneswari?', InfoChange, February 2009, https://bit.ly/2QaxwmN
6. Committee to Protect Journalists, '10 Most Censored Countries', https://bit.ly/1JqHwxu. Last accessed on 4 April 2019.

Chapter 1. Meeting Muivah

1. Biju M.R., *Mainstream Weekly*, LIII (36), 2015.

2.   Iralu K.D., 'The crucial facts of the Shillong Accord of 1975', *Morang Express*, 3 May 2017.
3.   'History of Naga National Movement', the *Sangai Express*, 7 May 2016.
4.   Ibid.

Chapter 2. Unravelling the ULFA

1.   Digambar Patowary/HT Correspondent, '9 new ULFA hit-men on most wanted list', 22 November 2009, https://bit.ly/2vgLcTW (last accessed on 22 April 2019).

Chapter 4. Diamond's Diary

1.   Digambar Patowary/HT Correspondent, '9 new ULFA hit-men on most wanted list', 22 November 2009, https:// bit.ly/2vgLcTW (last accessed on 22 April 2019).
2.   An abridged version of the diary was reported and published by the author in *Tehelka* magazine, 4(3), 2007.

Chapter 6. Mission Cobra

1.   Wasbir Hussain, 'Our land, our refugees', *The Hindu*, 26 May 2000.

Chapter 7. Media-savvy Militants

1.   D. Patowary, *The Hindustan Times*, 22 November 2009.

Chapter 8. Jungle Book

1.   Teresa Rehman, 'Rhino Killings: The Inside Story', *Tehelka*, 9 February 2008.
2.   Ibid.

Chapter 9. Reporting a Fake Encounter

1.   Teresa Rehman, 'Murder in plain sight', *Tehelka*, 8 August 2009, https://bit.ly/2YjeoGc

2.   Carol J. Williams, '"It's What I Do": A war-zone photographer's harrowing memoir', *Los Angeles Times*, 12 February 2015, https://lat.ms/2E0VrQT

3.   Anoo Bhuyan, 'CBI Will Destroy My Diaries, Alleges Manipur's "Killer Cop" on His Record of Killings', The Wire, 9 January 2018, https://bit.ly/2JaR61L